McGRAW-HILL SERIES IN SPEECH

Glen E. Mills Consulting Editor in General Speech

John J. O'Neill Consulting Editor in Speech Pathology

ARMSTRONG AND BRANDES **THE ORAL INTERPRETATION OF LITERATURE**

BAIRD **AMERICAN PUBLIC ADDRESSES**

BAIRD **ARGUMENTATION, DISCUSSION, AND DEBATE**

BAIRD AND KNOWER **ESSENTIALS OF GENERAL SPEECH**

BAIRD, BECKER, AND KNOWER **GENERAL SPEECH COMMUNICATION**

BLACK AND MOORE **SPEECH: CODE, MEANING, AND COMMUNICATION**

CARRELL AND TIFFANY **PHONETICS**

GIBSON **A READER IN SPEECH COMMUNICATION**

HAHN, LOMAS, HARGIS, VANDRAEGEN **BASIC VOICE TRAINING FOR SPEECH**

HASLING **THE MESSAGE, THE SPEAKER, THE AUDIENCE**

KAPLAN **ANATOMY AND PHYSIOLOGY OF SPEECH**

KRUGER **MODERN DEBATE**

OGILVIE **SPEECH IN THE ELEMENTARY SCHOOL**

OGILVIE AND REES **COMMUNICATION SKILLS: VOICE AND PRONUNCIATION**

POWERS **FUNDAMENTALS OF SPEECH**

REID **TEACHING SPEECH**

ROBINSON AND BECKER **EFFECTIVE SPEECH FOR THE TEACHER**

WELLS **CLEFT PALATE AND ITS ASSOCIATED SPEECH DISORDERS**

JOHN HASLING Foothill College, Los Altos Hills, California

the Message

the Speaker

the Audience

McGRAW-HILL BOOK COMPANY New York San Francisco St. Louis Dusseldorf
Johannesburg Kuala Lumpur London Mexico Montreal New Delhi
Panama Rio de Janeiro Singapore Sydney Toronto

THE MESSAGE, THE SPEAKER, THE AUDIENCE   This book was set in Video-comp Eterna by Datagraphics, Inc., and printed on permanent paper and bound by Peninsula Lithograph Company. The designer was Ronald Q. Lewton. The editors were Robert A. Fry, Ronald Q. Lewton, and Nancy Clark. Charles A. Goehring supervised production.

Printed in the United States of America.

Library of Congress catalog card number: 71-149715

1234567890 PEPE 7987654321   **07-026982-3**

Preface

There are many directions a speech course can take, and no single text can encompass them all. What is intended here is a compact basic text that covers the fundamental points. It is not designed to answer all the questions about the theory of communication or the techniques of public speaking—just the ones that are most often raised in a college-level course in the fundamentals of public speaking. My purpose is to provide a useful tool that students can keep at their elbows for quick and easy reference while they are preparing their speeches. The text is thus' directed to the beginning speech student, with the goal of helping him express himself clearly, succinctly, and with some degree of persuasiveness. It is also intended to make him aware of the responsibilities that are engendered by the art of persuasion.

The basic theme throughout is what I believe to be one of the most important principles in the discipline of speech—that the message is *the*

The message
The speaker
The audience

message as it is received. A student who considers that the nature of a message is determined by what he intended may never understand why he does not get the desired response. For this reason the text touches on the relevant aspects of behavioral psychology as well as rhetoric.

One of the difficult aspects of teaching speech is that there is so much a student needs to know before he can begin effectively. The usual dilemma is whether to start him on a speech before he is ready or to risk losing his interest by beginning the course with extensive lecture and discussion in preparation for the first speech. The first four chapters of this text provide the student with a step-by-step procedure so that he can begin almost immediately. The finer points can then be examined in greater detail as they come up—indeed, the best point at which to discuss them is as they come up in class. In this respect the instructor has a full range of flexibility for his own courses. At any point sections of other chapters may be either previewed or reviewed in terms of new information (the Study Guide at the end of each chapter provides a detailed summary of the contents), and supplementary readings may be assigned in any area in which greater depth is preferred.

Chapters 5 and 6 introduce the theory of argumentation and persuasion, in advance of the specifics for the speech to convince. There is just enough material to acquaint the student with some of the fundamental concepts and to show a clear connection between the theory and its application. Deductive reasoning is discussed to provide a conceptual framework for the prima facie case. Many of the factors in persuasion concern both the speaker and the audience, and parts of Chapter 6 may be introduced or reviewed at whatever point the instructor finds useful in his own classes.

One of the more controversial areas in the pedagogy of speech is instruction on delivery. The suggestions made in Chapters 8 and 9 are explicit, but they are not intended to be directive. Delivery is a highly individual thing, and instruction should not attempt to mold the student into a stereotype, but draw out the most effective characteristics of his style. It is hoped that these chapters will serve as a useful but flexible guide, leaving room for some degree of individual expression.

The last two chapters in the book focus on the audience. Since the student will spend more of his time in front of the podium that behind it, he should understand his responsibilities as a responding communicator as well as an originating communicator. Public speaking can be an effective means of communication only when the audience is alert and the speaker is skilled. This book is committed to the theory that both these qualities can be acquired.

Contents

The message
The speaker
The audience

CHAPTER 1

An introduction to communication

The use of sound to communicate is not unique to man. However, man is perhaps the only animal who can express abstract ideas in language; hence he is the only animal who can persuade. For thousands of years men have spoken to each other in hundreds of different languages, but they have never been satisfied with their ability to make themselves understood. Of all the forms of communication, language is the most explicit. It is also the most complex, and concern with rhetoric, the skill of using words, dates back to antiquity. As early as 3550 B.C. the Egyptians wrote on the principles of rhetoric. These writings had little practical application at the time, since Pharaoh was not a man to permit speeches in the public square. It was, in fact, another three thousand years before a society arose that was conducive to the study of rhetoric.

THE HISTORY OF RHETORIC

The first noteworthy text on public speaking was written by the Greek scholar Corax around 460 B.C. At this time the Greek city-states were experimenting with a democratic form of government, and a court system was established which allowed an accused man to plead his case before an assembly. However, he was not permitted to have anyone else speak for him; he had to address the assembly himself. Those who were not skilled in public speaking would go to teachers such as Corax for help in preparing their speeches. For the benefit of his students Corax worked out a system of organizing the speech and a method of argumentation. He was the first to postulate the three basic divisions we now call the *introduction,* the *body,* and the *conclusion.*

Corax and those who followed him were known as *sophists.* Some were highly principled and skilled. Others, such as Gorgias, were more concerned with eloquent style of delivery than with the truth of their arguments. They taught that the art of persuasion lay in the way a man spoke rather than in what he said. As more and more speakers began to employ grandiloquent oratory as a substitute for truth and knowledge, the sophists fell into poor repute. In fact the present meaning of the word "sophistry" is subtle reasoning deliberately intended to deceive. It is interesting to note that two other words from the same root are "sophisticated" and "sophomore."

This period of history, known as the Age of Pericles, saw many contributions to the art of rhetoric. Much of the philosophy articulated at that time formed the foundation of our present theories. One of the most influential scholars of this period was Isocrates, who maintained that truth was paramount in any oration, but that style was a legitimate means of persuading the listener to recognize that truth. Like Gorgias, he taught that a speech should be as well styled as the speaker could make it. However, he cautioned his students to employ only those proofs that they honestly believed:

> The same arguments we use in public we employ when we deliberate our own thoughts.

Oratory was classified at this time as *forensic,* or argumentative; *political,* or policy making; and *epideictic,* or eulogy. The father of forensics was Protagoras, who insisted that his students must be able to argue both sides of any issue. This is still a basic principle of debate. In most debate courses students are required to take first the affirmative and then the negative side of the proposition. The theory is that unless one is familiar with the arguments on both sides, he has no right to hold an opinion.

The most significant contribution to the art of rhetoric was made by Aristotle. The principles he outlined in 336 B.C. underlie everything that has been written since on the subject of public speaking, and his treatise *The Rhetoric* is still used as a text in colleges all over the world.[1] Aristotle provided us with the first model of the three basic components of communication—the *speaker*, the *message*, and the *audience*. His thesis was that all three of these components must be present for any communication to take place. This may seem an elementary observation, but as we will see, it is actually quite complex.

THE COMPONENTS OF COMMUNICATION

Aristotle's basic model of communication has since been expanded by the contributions of Sigmund Freud, John Dewey, Abraham Maslow, and most recently Marshall McLuhan. Whereas Aristotle viewed rhetoric as a formalized art, the modern theorists see it more in terms of human interaction. In this sense the three basic components are not separate and distinct entities. Rather, they are inextricably interwoven; communication is an inseparable sharing between speaker and listener.

The message   Let's look first at what it is that the speaker shares—the message. Messages do not necessarily consist of words. They may be conveyed by facial expression, gestures, physical appearance, tone of voice—all of which have nothing to do with the words we speak. In fact most of our messages are probably communicated at the *nonverbal* level, not only through the senses of sight and sound, but through the rest of the senses as well.

Even when words are used, they don't always convey a message. When someone asked Louis Armstrong to define jazz, he said

Man, if you got to ask what is it, you ain't never gonna get to know.

This is, in fact, one of the basic principles of semantics. The word is not the *thing;* the word is only a *symbol* for the thing. If the listener has had no experience of the thing the word represents, the word will have no

[1] *The Rhetoric and Poetics of Aristotle*, translated by W. Rhys Roberts, Modern Library, New York, 1954.

The message
The speaker
The audience

meaning to him. Even if he has experienced it, however, the precise meaning he attaches to the word will reflect his own individual experience. Since each person perceives the world from a slightly different angle, a word can rarely have exactly the same meaning for any two people. Of course there must be some common frame of reference, or people would be unable to communicate at all. However, the extent to which a word has the same meaning for two different people is only the extent to which the experiences they associate with it are similar.

In many cases a person will believe that he has understood the intended meaning of a word because he has a clear picture of what it means to him. This is particularly true of words that represent abstract concepts. Look at the abstract words in these lines from the Declaration of Independence:

> We hold these *Truths* to be self-evident, that all Men are created equal; that they are endowed by their Creator with certain unalienable *Rights;* that among these are *Life, Liberty,* and the Pursuit of *Happiness.*

There is no way to express such concepts except in words. But do the words really convey precise meanings? The listener will understand the words readily enough, but the meaning he attaches to them may be quite different from the meaning the speaker intended. This brings us to another important principle of semantics. The meaning itself is not in the words; it is only in the minds of those who use the words. Words do not *contain* meaning; they are merely the tools by which we attempt to *convey* it. And the more abstract the word, the less actual meaning it conveys.

Words are merely symbols for our own use in describing something, and of course a word has no effect on the thing it describes. Nevertheless, we often respond to words as though they endowed the thing itself with these qualities. We laud an institution that is described as "democratic" and condemn one described as "dictatorial" even though both may function in exactly the same way. We attach arbitrary word labels to things and then behave as though the label we have applied creates an actual difference in the thing we have applied it to.

The speaker   As if the verbal message were not sufficiently complex, the speaker adds a further dimension of complexity to it. In addition to the *primary message* he conveys with his words, he also conveys a message with his tone of voice, his appearance, and his gestures. This auxiliary message includes all the means of nonverbal communication a speaker employs to emphasize or augment his verbal message. He may dress in a certain way to project a specific image; he may smile to project friendliness; he may raise his voice to gain attention.

However, the message the speaker intends to convey is often affected by *secondary messages* which he did not intend and may be unaware of. He may have mannerisms that affect the audience's interpretation of what he is saying. His physical characteristics may influence his message in a way he has not considered. The same words spoken by a black speaker, or an attractive woman, or an elderly foreigner might have entirely different meanings to the audience. The speaker may have an advance reputation that causes the audience to attach a different significance to his words. All these factors influence the message the speaker actually conveys.

The audience   The same message, delivered by the same speaker, will not necessarily be interpreted the same way by different audiences. Their own backgrounds, attitudes, and beliefs will affect the message they receive. An audience may have strong religious or political convictions that provide them with a completely different frame of reference. Even such subtle factors as the time of day and the atmosphere of the occasion will have an effect. A tired audience may be impatient with jokes, whereas an audience in a frivolous mood may see almost anything as funny. Moreover, each person in the audience will have a slightly different interpretation of the words, and his response will be to the message as he interprets it. You can imagine the complexities in a large, heterogeneous audience.

We'll examine all these factors in detail later, but it should be clear by now that there is a lot more to public speaking than just opening your mouth and talking.

WHY STUDY PUBLIC SPEAKING?

You may be thinking to yourself right now, "But I'm not going to run for office; when will I ever have to stand behind a lectern and give formal speeches?" You may not. However, unless you end up living by yourself in a cave, you will be involved in some kind of communication situation about 70 percent of your waking hours. Most of it will be informal conversation, but much of it will be asking questions, reporting on something you have done, being interviewed, making requests to your employer, explaining things to your supervisor, discussing your ideas at meetings, and expressing your feelings to someone who is close to you. These situations require that you be clear and explicit, aware of your own feelings, and sensitive to the response of your listeners. All these qualities are examined and practiced in a speech course. Let's look at some of the specific things you can expect from this kind of course.

Learning to say what you mean The first thing a speech course will teach you is how to organize your ideas and your information so that you have something to say. Your aren't here to learn how to fill the air with meaningless sounds, so don't expect to get by on your "gift of gab." You will also learn how to say what you have to say clearly and succinctly, and in such a way that others will be interested in hearing it. As you have seen, your words are just one component of your message. You will learn specific skills and techniques for delivering it effectively and persuasively. Don't expect a speech course to teach you how to imitate someone else's dramatic style. Each person is different, and therefore each speaker is different. In this course you will learn to develop a speaking style that is uniquely your own.

Developing self-confidence Fear is nature's way of protecting you against getting into serious trouble, and it's a perfectly normal reaction to an unfamiliar situation. When the situation is no longer unfamiliar and you have gained some assurance of your ability to handle it, you lose your fear and begin to enjoy it. All too often someone who is well informed and has excellent ideas remains silent simply because he isn't sure how to verbalize his ideas or lacks the confidence to speak up. This is frustrating for him, but it is also a misfortune for those who are deprived of what he could have contributed. You will overcome much of your anxiety about speaking to a group of people once you understand the nature of the phenomenon, learn that you are not alone, and have a few successful experiences under your belt.

Learning more about yourself For many students this is the most important reason for taking a speech course. Up to this point you may have gotten very little feedback about the impression you make on other people. You probably know quite a bit about yourself, but primarily from the inside out. You may be surprised to discover that you come across to others as arrogant or sarcastic when you have no wish to convey such attitudes. You may learn other things about yourself as well. You can find out how much you know or don't know about your subject when you try to explain it to others. You may discover how you really feel about something when you have to formulate an opinion on it. You may find out that some of the opinions you had simply accepted as truths don't stand up under real

The message
The speaker
The audience

examination, and you may even change your opinions about some important matters. At least you will examine them carefully.

Learning to relate to others   In learning about the listener's role in the communication process you will become more aware of the feelings and attitudes of other people. You will learn to understand others better and thus be better able to relate to them. You will also become a better listener yourself, so that others will be able to relate more easily to you. In many of your classes you might go through the entire semester without even knowing the name of the person sitting next to you. In this class you will not only get to know everyone sitting around you, but you will learn about their backgrounds, their interests and accomplishments, and their attitudes and beliefs. It's not at all unusual for warm friendships to form under these circumstances. In addition to learning about this particular audience, you will learn some interesting things about audiences in general.

WHAT IS A GOOD SPEECH?

There are many areas of learning in which the desired results depend directly on mastery of the necessary skills and techniques. This is not so in public speaking. You could learn all the proper techniques and still not give a successful speech; and even if it were successful, there might be no concrete evidence of the results; and even if the results were immediately apparent, there might be considerable disagreement about whether they were desirable. This doesn't mean that there are no standards for distinguishing a good speech from a bad one. It means that in the art of public speaking, as in any other art, the results depend not on how well you apply the techniques, but on the use to which you put them. The results will also depend on the disposition of the people who are listening. There are times when an excellent speech may fail to move an audience; Lincoln's Gettysburg Address wasn't recognized as great until some time after it was delivered. There are also times when an exceedingly charismatic speaker may fire an audience to such enthusiasm that what he actually said is not evaluated objectively until many years later.

Generally an audience will respond to a speech on several different levels:

Artistic value. This would include the skillfulness of your organization, the imaginativeness of your material, your sentence structure and choice of words, and the eloquence of your language.

Intellectual value. This level concerns the content. You would be judged on the significance of your subject, the soundness of your ideas, and the validity of the evidence with which you support them.

Effectiveness of delivery. This level concerns the way in which you communicate your message to the audience. Part of the evaluation would be based on the clarity with which you speak, your use of timing, inflection, and vocal emphasis, the ease of your stance and effectiveness of your gestures, the rapport you establish with your audience, and the extent to which you capture and hold their attention.

Certainly a speech that is enthusiastically received by the audience can't be classified as a failure no matter how it falls short in other areas. Still, it wouldn't be fair for an instructor to grade a speech entirely on this basis. Some mediocre speeches are often applauded because the speaker is popular and well liked or because the audience agrees heartily with his views. Let's see if we can establish some more objective criteria for the speeches you will be giving in class:

The average speech. To meet the requirements for acceptability your speech should conform to the assignment; deal with a significant topic; follow an acceptable pattern of organization; have a clearly stated thesis; and be delivered extemporaneously.

The above-average speech. For an above-average rating your speech should also contain audience-interest factors; have a thoroughly developed introduction and conclusion; have well-organized areas of development; and be delivered with sincerity, enthusiasm, and good technique.

The superior speech. To be really superior your speech should include all the factors mentioned above. In addition, it should display evidence of thorough research coupled with creative thinking; it should deal with a challenging topic and show intellectual insight into this topic; it should demonstrate a superior ability to handle language; and it should be delivered effectively, with some element of style.

The below-average speech. A speech falls below acceptable standards if it is lacking in significant information; is poorly planned or contains irrelevant material; is read from notes instead of being delivered extemporaneously; or is inaudible.

The failing speech. A speech would be considered unacceptable if it clearly violated the assignment; had no element of purpose or significance; showed no evidence of preparation; or was plagiarized.

Now you have some idea of what you can expect from a course in speech and what will be expected of you in return. In the chapters that follow we'll examine the message, the speaker, and the audience.

QUESTIONS FOR DISCUSSION

1 Would you agree with Gorgias that people are more likely to be persuaded by the style of delivery than by the content of the speech? Can you think of any speakers who rely more on delivery than on the meaning of their words? To what extent do you feel it is ethical to use style as a means of achieving your end?

2 How would you define rock music to someone who had never heard it?

3 What do the words "truth," "rights," "life," "liberty," and "happiness" mean to you? Give some concrete examples to illustrate your meaning.

4 When someone attaches a meaning to your words that is not the meaning you intended, have you conveyed a message? If so, would you say that the message was the meaning you intended or the meaning he understood?

5 Would you say that a "gift of gab" is an advantage in communicating to others? In what ways might it be a handicap?

6 How can a speaker tell whether his speech has been effective? On what basis do you think a speech can best be evaluated? What would you say was the most important criterion for a good speech?

STUDY GUIDE

I. The study of rhetoric began with democratic government in the Greek city-states.
   A. The views of the sophists that eloquence of delivery was more important than content brought them into poor repute.
   B. Aristotle formulated the first basic model of communication.
II. The three essential components in all communication are the message, the speaker, and the audience.

The message
The speaker
The audience

A. The verbal message depends on the meaning attached to the words.
   1. The meaning intended by the speaker is never exactly the same as the meaning understood by the listener.
   2. The more abstract the concept, the less actual meaning is conveyed by the word that represents it.
B. The speaker conveys not just a verbal message, but auxiliary nonverbal messages and unintended secondary messages.
C. Regardless of the message conveyed by the speaker, the message received by the audience depends on their own backgrounds, attitudes, beliefs.
III. In a speech course you will learn to be more effective in all areas of communication.
IV. The criterion of a good speech is not necessarily its immediate effect on the audience.

The message
The speaker
The audience

CHAPTER 2

Selecting your subject and purpose

Public speaking is not the most effective means of communication. When one person is addressing a group he has little way of knowing whether he is really communicating with them. What's more, as the size of the group increases, the effectiveness of the communication decreases. Why, then, do college classes continue to use the traditional lecture system? One reason is economy, and as a matter of fact, as more money is made available classroom lectures are gradually giving way to small group discussions. However, public speaking, whether it is a classroom lecture, a presidential address, or a religious sermon, has one important advantage. It allows one person to share his knowledge with a large group in the

The message
The speaker
The audience

shortest time. This is why the art of public speaking has remained the cornerstone of communication for three millenniums, and why great men have devoted their lives to the study of it. It should be apparent, however, that unless the speaker is able to convey his information clearly and succinctly, he defeats the one important advantage that public speaking has over other methods of communication.

Public speaking is a *structured* communication situation, whereas conversation is *unstructured*. On this basis, group discussion, which falls between the two, might be classified as *semistructured*. Semistructured communication provides more give and take, a chance to clarify any misunderstandings, and the greater interest that results from participation. Structured communication is less time consuming, allows the speaker to convey more specific information, and allows him greater opportunity for persuasion. One type of communication situation is not superior to the other; each has its advantages and disadvantages, and the best choice depends entirely on the circumstances and the needs of the particular situation. In this book we deal primarily with structured communication.

THE PURPOSE OF YOUR SPEECH

In the eighteenth century the rhetorician George Campbell classified speeches according to the intent or purpose of the speaker. At one time these speech types were treated as distinct categories. In actuality, they overlap considerably. Nevertheless, the traditional broad categories are useful as a starting point:

The speech to entertain. This is sometimes called an *after-dinner speech* and is designed primarily to amuse the audience. It generally consists of a series of humorous references worked around a central theme, and any real information that may be included is only incidental. This is the kind of speech you might hear at a victory banquet or at the senior class revue, when the audience is relaxed and in a frivolous mood.

The speech to inform. This is sometimes called an *expository speech* because it is designed to expose information rather than to advocate some particular point of view. The topic should be a noncontroversial one, so that the audience does not become involved in taking issue with the speaker. This is the kind of speech that would be given as a report to a committee, where the speaker's responsibility is not to make a decision, but to provide information so that the committee can make a decision. It is also the kind of speech you would expect from a classroom lecturer.

The speech to convince. This is a speech designed to persuade the audience to some point of view to which they may be opposed or apathetic. Both emotional and logical appeals are employed to bring the audience around to the speaker's way of thinking. This is the kind of speech you would hear in a debate, in a courtroom, or in a political campaign.

The speech to stimulate. This is a speech designed to reinforce an attitude that the audience already holds. It is effective only with an audience that is in basic agreement with the speaker to begin with. You would expect to hear this kind of speech at a rally or at a testimonial dinner.

The speech to entertain and the speech to stimulate are highly specialized and perhaps the most difficult kinds to give. You may want to discuss them in class, but we won't deal with them separately here.

Often the general purpose of your speech will be selected for you. You may be asked to help campaign for your class president or to report on some research project. Sometimes your subject will be assigned—say, you have been asked to talk about student housing—and you will have to pick your general purpose. In either case, you will find that the general purposes overlap considerably. You can't give a speech to stimulate until your audience is convinced, and to convince them you must first provide them with information. You will probably also employ some aspect of entertainment or humor in any speech to hold the attention of your audience.

In addition, the intent of the speaker is not always the same as the response of the audience. For example, a speaker may intend to be informative in discussing the theory of evolution. However, suppose he is speaking to an audience that believes in a fundamentalist interpretation of the Bible and considers this topic highly controversial. The speaker intends to be informative, but his audience will respond to what he says as an attempt to persuade them to some other view. How then should the speech be classified—as informative or persuasive? Most writers would agree that audience response is paramount; the speech would have to be classified as persuasive if that's the way the message was received. You may think you are "just giving the facts," but your listeners will have their own response to the facts you select, regardless of your intended purpose.

YOUR AUDIENCE

Later on we'll delve more deeply into the subject of audience analysis. For now, however, what about the particular audience to whom you will be speaking in class? It will vary, of course, from one class to another. Each listener will have a slightly different background and frame of reference —and there may even be some major differences. Many instructors have students give autobiographical speeches in the early part of a speech course. If any are given in your class, listen to them carefully. These will give you your best clues about the individuals that make up your audience. We can begin, however, with some broad generalities about college students as a group:

The college student is usually above the national norm in intelligence. This means he has a good vocabulary and a fairly broad knowledge in academic fields. Be careful that you don't talk down to him, as if you were explaining to a child. The information you present should be on the same level you would want him to present it to you.

The college student usually has a greater curiosity and a broader range of interests than the national norm. This means that you should be able to hold his interest even if he has no specific knowledge of your topic. You should be able to speak to any college student on music, art, drama, politics, history, literature, economics, science, or philosophy, whether the subject is related to his own field or not.

The college student is young, usually between the ages of eighteen and twenty-six. He will most likely be familiar with the subculture of youth—the language, music, personalities, issues, and characteristics of your own generation. He is likely to be more aware and more critical of the social problems that the older generation has created, or ignored, or failed to cope with. He is going to be particularly concerned about problems that will affect him twenty years from now—overpopulation, pollution of the environment, and the arms race.

The college student is usually more objective than the population as a whole. He is less set in his ways and more willing to at least consider new methods of doing things. He is also more likely to see fallacies in argumentation and to want facts in support of contentions. He is just as emotional as anyone else, but slightly less likely to be swayed by emotionalism alone.

There are certainly many exceptions, but let's proceed on the assumption that this is a profile of your audience. You may want to discuss in class the kinds of adjustments that would have to be made in your presentation when you have a different kind of audience.

THE SUBJECT OF YOUR SPEECH

Now that you have some idea of your audience, what will you talk to them about? Let's suppose at this point that your general purpose is an informative speech.

Deciding on a general area of discussion   There are numerous sources you can look to for help in deciding on general areas of discussion—books you have read; movies, plays, and television shows you have seen; courses you have taken. If you don't come up with any ideas, there are reference books designed especially for this purpose.[1] You might think first in terms of your own experiences—trips you have taken, places you have lived, hobbies you have had, people you have met. Maybe you have worked as a forest ranger, or you collect South American folk music, or you've lived through a power failure, a flood, or an earthquake.

Your instructor may ask you to select a topic in your academic field, one that requires library research as well as personal experience in such areas as psychology, sociology, history, government, economics, anthropology, or geology. If so, take advantage of this opportunity to clarify for yourself what you have learned in other courses. You have probably observed that things often become clearer in your own mind when you have to explain them to someone else. You may find in the process that your difficulty in explaining something to another person stems from the fact that you don't really understand it as well as you thought you did. Bear in mind that topics dealing with mathematics and the sciences may be completely mystifying to listeners who have no grounding in the basic principles relating to these areas; you must be prepared to fill in the fundamentals.

There are a few things to keep in mind in selecting the topic of your speech:

It must be significant. Don't waste your time, your instructor's time, and the time of your audience with idle chatter. The right to speak carries with it the responsibility of having something worthwhile to say.

It must be of interest to the audience. You haven't been given the floor to show off your knowledge or reminisce about your past experiences. You are there to meet the needs of the audience, not your own need to speak.

[1] For example, Zebulan Vance Hooker, *An Index for Writers and Speakers,* Scott, Foresman, Chicago, 1965.

The message
The speaker
The audience   15

It must be something you are enthusiastic about. The most common reason for the failure of a speech is the speaker's lack of enthusiasm. Pick a topic that will really turn you on. The chances are that it will do the same for the audience.

Bringing your topic into focus   Don't overestimate the amount of material you can cover in the six to eight minutes you will have for your speech. You won't be able to discuss the whole field of coin collecting, but you should be able to discuss certain rare coins from one particular country. Millions of words have been written in the field of psychology; you have time for less than a thousand of them, but you might be able to cover the uses for aptitude tests in that length of time. How closely you limit your topic may depend on the depth of your knowledge in that limited area. One student spoke for eight minutes on the operation of one valve on a Scuba tank. As a general rule, you should narrow your topic as much as you can without having to pad your speech or repeat yourself.

Possible areas of development   Remember that when you start organizing your material you are going to have to break your topic down into more specific areas of development. After you have picked your topic, ask yourself, "What are some specific aspects of this topic that I can cover?" In a speech on skydiving, for instance, you might discuss packing the parachute, exiting from the plane, maneuvering in the air, and landing. These subtopics will become your main headings when you begin writing your outline. If you can't think of any subtopics, the chances are that your topic is too limited, and you should try to broaden it. For example, a speech on the use of chopsticks might be expanded to include other oriental eating utensils.

YOUR PURPOSE STATEMENT

The first step in preparing your speech is to write out *one statement* that tells clearly and concisely what your speech is about. Your purpose statement, or thesis, should be tentative until you begin to research your topic and find out whether the information you need is available. There are some general rules for constructing your purpose statement:

It should be a complete sentence, phrased the way you normally speak. This is approximately the way you are going to say it when you deliver your speech.

It should be a statement, not a question. You may use a rhetorical question to lead
    into your purpose statement, but the statement itself should be a declara-
    tive sentence.

Phrase it so that it focuses on the audience, not on you. Remember that this is a
    college speech class, not "show and tell." If you are going to talk about
    your trip to Europe, don't begin with

> Let me tell you about my recent trip to Europe.

Turn it toward your audience:

> If you plan to visit Europe, there are points of interest that you
> shouldn't miss.

Here are a few examples of purpose statements, some from personal
experience:

> There is no greater thrill than shooting the rapids of the Colorado River.
>
> Dinner in a Japanese home is not just a meal; it is an expression of a
> culture.
>
> Collecting folk music from other countries raises some interesting
> points about our own Country and Western music.
>
> Sports-car driving is a challenge to the mind as well as to the driving
> skill.
>
> Dog training teaches you a lot of things about people as well as dogs.

and some from academic areas:

> Most geologists agree that California will experience a major earth-
> quake before the end of the century.
>
> Psychologists have demonstrated that human attitudes can be
> changed through the process of conditioning.
>
> The urban renewal is one way that the federal government hopes to
> save the cities.
>
> Investing in the stock market is risky, but it can also be profitable.
>
> The American Negro has played a significant role in all phases of
> United States history.

Constructing your purpose statement is one of the most important
steps in preparing your speech. If you have not crystallized exactly what

you plan to discuss in one carefully thought out statement, you may end up confusing yourself as well as your audience.

QUESTIONS FOR DISCUSSION

1 If public speaking is not the most effective means of communication, what is? Should colleges and universities abandon the lecture method altogether and substitute group discussion? How informative are the conversations you have with friends?

2 Is it possible to give an informative speech that contains no element of persuasion? If not, where would you draw the line in classifying a speech as informative?

3 Would you agree that public speaking provides more opportunity for persuasion than group discussion? If so, in what way? When you argue with a friend are you really trying to convince him, or are you just expounding your views?

4 Do you agree that college students tend to be more objective than other groups? How would you describe the characteristics of a college audience? Does the description given in the text fit the students in your speech class?

5 Do you feel that a speech course is easier for someone who has had a wide variety of personal experiences? To what extent do you feel that reading can substitute for personal experience?

6 On what basis would you decide that a topic was significant and would interest your audience? Do you think you could interest them in a topic simply because it was of great interest to you?

STUDY GUIDE

I. Public speaking is structured communication.
   A. It allows a speaker to convey the most information to the greatest number in the least amount of time.
   B. It provides the greatest opportunity for persuasion.
II. The first step in preparing a speech is to determine its general purpose.
   A. A speech may be designed primarily to entertain, to inform, to convince, or to stimulate.

    B. The purpose of a speech is determined ultimately by the purpose to which the audience responds.
III. The audience you will be addressing has some general characteristics you should take into consideration.
IV. Your topic may be based on personal experience or on some academic area.
    A. Narrow down your topic as much as possible without having to pad.
    B. Consider possible areas of development.
V. Your purpose sentence should crystallize exactly what you plan to discuss.

CHAPTER 3

Gathering the information

Once you have selected a topic you can talk about enthusiastically, you will have to consider just what you want to say about it. It isn't hard to fill up eight minutes with words; it is hard, however, to present specific and meaningful information in this length of time. If your topic is one that you know a lot about, you probably won't be able to cover everything that you know. You will have to decide which things are the most important and then figure out the best way to discuss them in the length of time you have. This is why a short speech is often harder to give than a long one. Woodrow Wilson once told a friend that he didn't have time to prepare a five-minute speech, but he was ready at a moment's notice to speak for an hour.

If your assignment is a speech based on some personal experience, you may not have to do any library research. Frequently, however, you will

The message
The speaker
The audience

20

be asked to support your topic with documented information. The following steps will not only save you time in the long run, but will provide you with a technique that you can use for other research projects.

RESEARCHING YOUR SUBJECT

One reason for getting an early start on your research is to find out whether there is actually enough information available on the topic you have selected. If not, you may have to pick another one. It may be that your topic is so esoteric that your library has nothing on it. It may also be that your thesis is one that can't be supported.

Indexes to research material   You may never have occasion to become familiar with all the indexes to research material, but there are some basic tools that all college students should know how to use:

The Readers' Guide to Periodical Literature. This index is arranged according to topic, with cross references to the various subtopics. It will direct you to information appearing in the more popular periodicals, such as the *Saturday Review of Literature, Atlantic Monthly, Time,* and *Newsweek.*

The Social Sciences and Humanities Index. This index, also arranged and cross-indexed by topic, will direct you to more specialized professional journals in the social sciences, such as the *Journal of Philosophy* and *Political Science Quarterly.*

The New York Times Index. This is an excellent index for current affairs. In most libraries copies of the *New York Times* are available on microfilm.

The Education Index. This index will refer you to professional journals dealing with the various aspects of education.

Psychological Abstracts. This index is handy if your library has it. It covers the professional journals in this field and also gives a brief résumé of each of the articles.

General reference works   For general background information on historical or scientific topics your best source is the encyclopedias. You are probably familiar with the *Americana,* the *Brittanica,* and *Collier's,* but there are also more specialized works, such as the *Encyclopedia of Social Sciences,* the *Encyclopedia of American History,* the *Encyclopedia of the American Negro,* and the *Encyclopedia of Associations.*

For information about people you can consult *Current Biography*, *American Biography*, *Who's Who*, *Who's Who in America*, *Who's Who in the West*, and *Who Was Who*. For statistical information look in the *World Almanac*, the *Information Please Almanac*, *Facts on File*, or *Statistical Abstracts of the United States*.

After you have checked all these works, ask your librarian for further help. He is there to assist you, but he will be more willing if you can tell him that you have already looked in the conventional places.

This may seem like a lot of work, but no one said it was supposed to be easy. If you find that your research takes quite a bit of time and effort, then you are probably going about it in the right way.

Recording what you read   You may do a lot of reading in preparation for your speech and find later that there is little evidence of it in your results. Don't count on remembering what you have read. You may remember the gist of it, but when you start putting your speech together you will find that you don't have the specific information you need to support your contentions. And even if you do recall that there was some specific piece of information, the chances are that you won't remember just where you saw it. *Take notes as you read*. Keep track of the details in any example, so that in each case you have a record of *who* was involved, *what* happened, and *where*, *when*, and *how* it happened.

SUPPORTING YOUR ASSERTIONS

Look again at the purpose statements we discussed in Chapter 2. All of them are *assertions*. That is, they are fairly broad general statements which will have to be supported by the substance of your speech. When you begin developing your outline, your main headings will also be in the form of assertions. Here are three typical examples:

The Constitution places many restrictions on the power of the President of the United States.

The Supreme Court has forced local law-enforcement agencies to abide by strict regulations in arrest procedures.

Poverty is a serious problem in the United States.

These statements might be true in general. However, they are no more than assertions until you provide specific examples of what you mean. These particular assertions, for instance, might be supported as follows:

The Constitution places many restrictions on the power of the President of the United States. Article I, Section 8, gives to Congress the power to declare war and to raise and support armies; Article II, Section 2, says that treaties made by the President must be ratified by two-thirds of the Senate.

The Supreme Court has forced local law-enforcement agencies to abide by strict regulations in arrest procedures. In the Escobedo decision the Supreme Court ruled that a man is entitled to see his lawyer before he is interrogated, and that he must be advised of his constitutional right to remain silent if he wants to.

Poverty is a serious problem in the United States. The President's Council of Economic Advisers had defined poverty as the condition of a family of four living in an urban community on an income of less than $3,000 a year. By these standards, 15 to 20 million Americans are presently living in a condition of poverty.

The assertions are now backed up by specific examples. Let's take a closer look at the kinds of support that have been used.

Quotations   Instead of just saying that the Constitution restricts the President's powers, tell your audience just what the Constitution says on this point. Often it is better to paraphrase than to recite a long quotation in full, but be sure your paraphrase accurately reflects the original meaning. If you excerpt brief passages from long quotations, you must also be careful not to distort the meaning by quoting out of context. In any case, whether you paraphrase or quote verbatim, always give the source. One reason of course, is to avoid plagiarism—passing off someone else's thoughts as your own. The other reason is to give your statement the weight of authority. Any quotations you use should be selected from sources that are authoritative in the area you are discussing. However, it is the audience who must recognize the source as authoritative. If you are quoting an expert who is not well known, be sure you explain what qualifies him as an expert in this area.

Specific cases   The Supreme Court has made many decisions regarding arrest procedures. Don't make your audience guess which ones you are referring to. It is your examples that will show them whether local law-enforcement agencies have in fact been forced to abide by strict regulations. They will also be able to determine whether or not you know what you are talking about.

Definitions   If you are claiming that poverty is a serious problem, you have to define exactly what you mean by "poverty." In this context it is merely an abstract word, and without a definition your statement has no clear meaning. For that matter, not only do abstract words need to be defined, but so do technical terms. For instance, if you were giving a speech on radio broadcasting and referred to a combo man, you would have to explain that in this field a "combo man" is someone who works as a combination announcer and engineer. The best time to define a term is immediately after you use it.

Facts and figures   Think of the people you know whose opinions you listen to. They are probably the ones who have the facts when they make a statement. They don't have to rely on generalities or back up what they say with guesses; they know how many or what percentage, and usually they can tell you where they got their information. The same is true in public speaking. The effective speaker knows how many people are considered to be in a state of poverty, or how many men are stationed in Vietnam, or what the gross national product was last year. This doesn't mean that you should bore your audience with an encyclopedic listing of dry facts and figures (you probably know people who do this too). Facts and figures should be used like seasoning—with discretion.

Whenever you use figures or statistics, always give the source so that your audience can judge for themselves whether the figures are reliable. In some cases, in fact, the source is as important as the figures themselves. One point to bear in mind is that large numbers will be difficult for your audience to remember. It helps to round them off to the nearest thousand or million, and if you can, to compare them to some smaller amount. For example, instead of simply stating that the national debt is over $300 billion dollars, explain that this equals $1500 for every man, woman, and child in the United States. If the figures are extremely important, it's a good idea to write them on the chalkboard as you give them.

Some of your support material will come from your research, and some will probably come from your own experience. Regardless of the source, there are some general rules to consider in selecting your examples:

Vary your methods of support. Just as a speech containing only statistical examples would be dull, so would one that relied entirely on quotations, or entirely on definitions. Be sure that you have different kinds of supporting material.

Be selective. In the six to eight minutes you have for your speech you won't be able to give a long dissertation. You will have to limit yourself to just the examples you have time for, so be sure you pick the best ones. This doesn't mean you should stop collecting information as soon as you have eight minutes' worth. Gather all the information you can, and save the rest of your examples for any discussion that might come up afterward.

Always use more than one source. You may be tempted to base your speech on some particular article that you have found interesting. Even if you put the material in your own words, basing your speech on someone else's work is still plagiarism. Aside from the ethics of such a practice, it is technically illegal. You place your own reputation in jeopardy; moreover, you add nothing to your own learning, and those in the audience who are familiar with the original material will find your rehash of it old hat.

Be prepared to change your thesis if necessary. The success of your speech will depend to a large extent on the interest you create with your examples. Don't blind yourself to interesting material just because you have already decided on your thesis. In the course of your research you may come across an excellent example that is relevant but doesn't quite fit in. You may be able to reorient your thesis so that you can use it. Sometimes, in fact, it isn't a bad idea to reverse the usual procedure and develop your thesis after you have seen what examples are available.

DEVELOPING YOUR SUBJECT

As you are gathering your information you should give some thought to how you are going to present it to your audience. There are a number of ways in which you might develop your subject.

Explanation   This is one of the most common ingredients in the speech to inform. Explaining a process, a procedure, or a phenomenon, however, doesn't mean dazzling the audience with your knowledge; it means communicating your knowledge. Your audience has to understand what you are telling them. To make sure they understand your explanation begin with what they already know, and then take them through the new material step by step, with clarity and simplicity. If you are explaining how a temperature inversion results in severe smog conditions, explain the entire phenomenon, starting with the basic principle that warm air rises.

Analogy and comparison   Research has shown that people absorb new information only by relating it to the knowledge they already have. Instead of leaving it to the audience to tie in your information with what they already know, show them the relationship yourself by giving specific analogies and comparisons. They are more likely to grasp the difference between voltage and current if you make the analogy that when one end of a pipe full of water is squeezed, the amount of water (voltage) remains the same but the pressure (current) is increased. Sometimes the comparisons people draw in their own minds will hinder rather than aid their understanding. For example, since most people tend to compare wolves with dogs, they will usually view the differences as a sign of the wolf's wildness. However, the behavior of your baby wolf will not seem so foreign to them when you point out familiar examples of the same behavior in kittens. Carefully considered analogies and comparisons can make your explanations more interesting as well as more understandable.

Narration   This form of development can be either very interesting or very boring, depending on your skill as a narrator. If you have a good story to tell, tell it—but keep it short and to the point. Be sure it is relevant, and not just an excuse for personal reminiscences or tooting your own horn. It's a good idea to save some kind of punch line for the end of your tale, and then follow it with a clear indication of how the story relates to your main idea.

Description   This is one of the most difficult forms of development to handle well. Like narration, skillfully created word pictures can do a great deal for your speech, but description that falls flat can be an embarrassing venture. Whether you are describing the natural beauties of Yosemite or the blight of an urban slum area, your audience should be able to see the sight as you saw it and share the image you have in your own mind. Unless you are sure you can accomplish this, you are better off avoiding descriptions altogether. If you do use them, be particularly careful that you don't fall back on clichés or such trite utterances as "It was really beautiful."

There is one more factor you will have to consider when you start putting your material together. You're going to have a pretty hard time holding the attention of your audience. Aside from the fact that you are new at all this, there is one big audience factor that you don't have going for you. Your instructor can hold the attention of the class because his material will be covered on the final examination; other speakers may hold attention because the audience has come specifically to hear them, or because they have great prestige in their fields. You don't have this edge. Your audience is there because they have to be. They know they won't be held responsible for anything you say, so unless your material is interesting they don't have any real reason to listen. Look back over the notes you have made so far and see if your examples include the following interest factors:

Humor   You know yourself that humor is a good means of getting your audience with you. Why? Because in responding with a laugh they become active participants in the communication process. This doesn't mean you have to be a comedian; you are giving a speech to inform, not a speech to entertain. However, a humorous reference will do a lot to relax both you and your audience.

Suspense   Since the tales of Scheherezade suspense has been used as a device to pique the listener's interest and hold his attention right through to the end. If you can build suspense effectively, the audience will be eager to hear how your story comes out. As with narration, however, be sure you can do it well, and that any such device is clearly tied to your main point.

Uniqueness   The extent to which you can select unusual examples to support your main idea depends largely on the nature of your topic. Topics such as space travel, buried treasure, or evidence of the supernatural afford more opportunities in this respect than, say, household plumbing fixtures—although even here some possibilities come to mind. One student described a study showing that a certain kind of worm could be conditioned more easily after it had been fed another worm that had already been conditioned; she wound up with the thought that perhaps students could learn a subject more easily if the instructor were first carved up and served to the class.

Familiar references   Have you ever been daydreaming during a lecture and then snapped back to attention when the speaker mentioned the name of a friend, or a place you had visited, or an incident you were involved in? This is a phenomenon that good speakers recognize as an effective interest factor. The trick is to select a reference that will have a ring of familiarity for your audience. You can make some pretty good guesses on the basis of other speeches made in class, characteristics of the instructor or other students, or local places and events.

Vital statements   It is a fact of human nature that the degree of interest aroused by any statement is generally in direct proportion to its pertinence for the individual listener. People pay attention to the things that are going to affect them directly. This is why newspapers often devote more space to local news than to world events. A discussion of inflation in terms of the gross national product or the cost-of-living index won't rouse your audience to a feverish pitch of excitement, but they are likely to take notice if you bring the point closer to home with some specifics about the price of cigarettes or hamburgers. They will probably find the effect of smog on their own life expectancy of more vital concern than its effect on the world's grain crop.

One final point to bear in mind is that people can listen faster than you can talk. Studies have shown that the normal attention span is only a matter of *seconds*. This means you will not only have to capture the attention of your audience, you will have to keep on recapturing it every few seconds. No one is going to compel your audience to listen to you. Their attention will depend entirely on what you say and how you say it.

QUESTIONS FOR DISCUSSION

1 Would you say that one person's opinion is just as good as another's? If not, what is it that makes a difference?

2 There's an old saying that "figures never lie, but liars sure can figure." In what ways can figures and statistics be misleading? Can you give some examples?

3 Are you more inclined to believe a statement when it is made with confidence and assurance? When you hear two conflicting statements, how do you decide which is true?

4 What is it that makes some speeches interesting and others dull? Can you think of other interest factors besides the ones mentioned in the text?

5 Does the attention of the audience depend entirely on what is said and how it is said? What are some things that might interfere with audience attention?

STUDY GUIDE

I. Review the material that is available on the topic you have selected.
  A. If you can't find sufficient material, select another topic.
  B. Become familiar with the standard reference works.
    1. Indexes to research material refer the reader to journal articles.

      2. General reference works provide historical, scientific, and autobiographical background information.
  C. Take notes on what you read, including specific details and source of information.
II. Use concrete examples to support your assertions.
  A. Quote only from experts in the subject area you are discussing.
  B. Give specific cases to illustrate any point you discuss.
  C. Define any technical terms peculiar to the field.
  D. Always give the source of your figures and statistics.
III. Develop your subject.
  A. Be sure you provide the necessary background material in explanations.
  B. Use analogies and comparisons for both clarity and interest.
  C. Avoid narration and description unless you know you can handle them well.
IV. Include factors designed specifically for audience interest.

CHAPTER 4

Organizing your material

If you want to get something done, ask the busiest person you know to do it. Somehow the student who is a member of the college council, president of the debating club, chairman of the finance committee, and out for track is always the one who can work another project into his schedule. He can pack more into a day because he has learned to organize his time. By the same token, some people can pack more information into their speeches than others. The one who speaks the longest is not necessarily the one who says the most. Much material can be carried in a short time if it is clearly stated and properly organized. Good organization is essential to effective speaking for three reasons: It will allow you to say the most in

The message
The speaker
The audience

the time that you have; it will permit your audience to follow you more easily and retain what you say; and it will minimize the risk of forgetting what you plan to cover. Being armed with a definite sequence of ideas may also ease the stage fright that arises from fear of forgetting your material.

An outline is the most effective means of organizing your material. Once you learn to outline well, you will find it easier and more useful than writing out a complete script because the structure of your speech will be apparent at a glance. Before you begin, make a careful, objective evaluation of all your material. Does it support a central idea? Is it concrete and significant? Will your audience be interested in it? If you get a "no" answer to any of these questions, start over.

PREPARING YOUR ROUGH DRAFT

Your outline must be legible, so plan from the beginning to copy it over. Don't expect to get all your ideas and information down on paper in a neat well-organized fashion the first time. You will have to cross things out, change headings, and add notations in the margin—at least you will if you are at all concerned about what you are doing. If you plan from the outset on starting with a rough draft and then recopying it, you will be less reluctant to make the necessary improvements on your first effort.

Rewrite your purpose statement   You wrote your purpose statement before you began your research, but remember that it was only tentative. Look back over Chapter 2, and then write your purpose statement in more or less final form. Make sure it is clearly stated and fully *qualified*. Don't be afraid to use enough words to say what you mean. It isn't enough to say

Today I would like to talk about coin collecting.

This statement is not qualified; that is, it places no restrictions on the vast area of coin collecting. You might improve on it by saying

Coin collecting is not only a fascinating hobby, but it can also be a profitable one.

Now you have introduced your subject, conveyed your attitude toward it, and suggested at least one point of development—profitability.

Add a presummary to your purpose statement   When you were deciding on your subject you made note of some possible areas of development (at least you should have; see Chapter 2). With these in mind, write your presummary; that is, summarize what you plan to cover to give your audience a preview of what is to come. The presummary will also help you organize the information for yourself. If you begin by telling the audience what you are going to tell them, you are less likely to leave out material you had planned to include. You have committed yourself to particular areas of development.

Suppose your purpose sentence was

Learning to play the guitar is not as difficult as you may think.

This states your topic and expresses your attitude toward it, but it doesn't tell your audience much about what you are going to cover. It would be better to add another sentence:

To get off to a good start there are two things you need to know—how to select a guitar and how to select a teacher.

This gives the audience a clue to your organizational pattern and tells them what they can expect in your speech. The presummary becomes part of your purpose statement, but it need not be written word for word on your outline. It would probably look something like this:

Learning to play the guitar is not as difficult as you may think.
    A. Selecting a guitar
    B. Selecting a teacher

Write your main headings   The main headings constitute the foundation of your outline. These are the broad generalizations or assertions that your specific examples are intended to support. Write them in complete sentences, in the language you normally use when you speak. You don't have to memorize them. Once you have written them out in full-sentence form on your outline, they will come back to you with more familiarity when you deliver the speech.

Your main headings should be consistent with what you said in the presummary, and in the same order. In other words, follow the pattern of organization you said you were going to use. In the speech on the guitar, for example, your main headings might be in this form:

    I. The best guitar for you is not necessarily the most expensive one.
    II. Before you spend any money on lessons, find out the qualifications of the teacher.

You will confuse your audience if you reverse the order or if you include areas that were not referred to in your presummary.

Your main headings should say something meaningful about your topic. The audience is more likely to remember the main ideas of a speech than the specific details; be sure that your main point is clear. Instead of saying

> I'm going to give you some statistics about unemployment.

it would be better to say

> The rate of unemployment has continued to decline over the past decade.

Your main headings should follow some pattern. The particular pattern that is best for your speech depends on your purpose and the effect you want to achieve. No matter which arrangement you select, however, be sure that all your headings follow the *same* pattern. Don't confuse your audience and yourself by starting out on one basis and then switching to another.

There are several heading patterns with which you should be familiar. Consider them carefully, and then decide which arrangement best suits your needs.

The topical pattern. This is the most common arrangement; it consists merely of breaking the speech down into its component parts, as we did with the speech on the guitar. Here is another example:

I. The legislative branch of our government makes the law.
II. The judicial branch interprets the law.
III. The executive branch is the one that carries out the law.

The chronological pattern. This is a good arrangement for explaining a process or for discussing some progression:

I. The first step in constructing a patio is to make your forms.
II. The next step is to pour the concrete.
III. The final step is to smooth the surface.

The spatial pattern. Some topics can best be discussed in terms of physical areas. For example, recreational facilities might be organized according to geographic area:

I. The coastal region offers swimming, surfing, and deep-sea fishing.
II. The mountain areas offer skiing in the winter and back packing in the summer.

They might also be discussed in terms of different levels of altitude.

The problem-solution pattern. This type of arrangement might be used for a speech to convince, where the speaker describes a problem and then shows his solution for it:

    I. Polluted air is not just a nuisance, it's a killer.
    II. One of the major contributing causes is the automobile.
    III. The only way to end the smog problem is to eliminate the internal-combustion engine.

The indirect pattern. This pattern would be used where a hostile audience must be persuaded to accept the speaker's viewpoint. The speaker begins with the point that is easiest for them to accept and then progresses to the controversial point of his thesis:

    I. The federal government in a democracy has a responsibility for the well-being of the citizens it represents.
    II. Many of those people who are in a condition of poverty are there for reasons beyond their control.
    III. The federal government should provide a minimum guaranteed income for all citizens.

Support and develop your main headings   Main headings cannot stand alone. Since they are merely assertions, you have to support them by specific examples. No matter what types of support material you use, the important thing to remember is that the examples must be relevant to the main heading. By the same token, the main heading must clearly govern all the information under it. At times you may have to reword your main heading so that it covers all the examples you want to include, or perhaps narrow it down so that it relates more specifically to the examples you do have.

When you write your outline, number your main headings. Then, when you add your support material, letter each point and indent it under the main heading that governs it. If you have further subpoints, these should also be numbered or lettered and indented under the statement they are intended to support:

    I. One of the animals that is becoming extinct is the polar bear.
      A. Josef Van De Brugge: immense numbers in 1670
        1. Estimated 250,000
        2. Seen as far south as middle Canada
      B. Steady decline in population since eighteenth century
        1. William Barents: 1,000 seen slain in 1830
        2. 125 per month killed by one hunter
        3. Population now about 12,000

    (a)   Only 50 seen by Eskimos in a lifetime

    (b)   Will be extinct by year 2000

Write your conclusion   Studies show that your conclusion is more likely to be remembered than what you have said in the body of your speech. Utilize this important portion of the speech to its best advantage. If you have held your audience, they will be with you at this point. If you haven't, they will at least be listening for signs that you are about to finish. One way or the other, however, this is the point at which you will have their attention, so make the most of it. If your purpose is to convince your audience or to stimulate them to action, your conclusion might be planned to win them over. Think of some of the famous concluding lines:

Give me liberty or give me death.

You shall not crucify mankind upon a cross of gold.

In any speech your conclusion should focus attention on your main idea. You should still be talking at the end of your speech about what you said in your purpose statement. Let's look at some of the methods you might use:

The summary. One of the most common ways of concluding a speech is to summarize your main idea. This might simply be a restatement of your thesis. If it has been a long speech with many complicated points, you may want to reiterate each of the important ones. Your summary should be long enough to make your point, but be careful not to drag it out so that it loses its punch.

The quotation. This can be an effective method of concluding a speech if the quotation is well phrased and apt. You might get some ideas from *Bartlett's Familiar Quotations,* which is indexed according to subject and author.

The illustrative anecdote. This can be effective as a conclusion if you are a good storyteller. The same factors apply as for narration. Make sure any anecdote you use is to the point and that you are able to tell it clearly and succinctly.

However you decide to end your speech, make sure you have planned it. Don't expect a good conclusion to just happen. Usually it doesn't—and there you are with nothing more to say and no exit line. Plan your exit line, so that you wind up on a strong, dynamic note.

Write your introduction   If your conclusion is important, your introduction is even more important. The introduction to a speech has several specific functions:

It should orient the audience to your topic. Let your audience know exactly what you are going to tell them. Be careful not to mislead them by including irrelevant material in your introduction.

It should establish the importance of your topic. The importance of your topic may or may not be self-evident. Accident prevention in the home, for example, may not seem too significant until you point out that household accidents cause more deaths each year than automobile and airplane accidents combined.

It should establish rapport with your audience. It is often true that people are not only more willing to accept what you say, but also more willing to believe you if they like you as a person. In those first few seconds your audience is sizing you up, so make the best impression you can. If you want your audience to like you, let them know that you like them.

It should capture the attention of your audience. Before you can tell your audience anything, they have to be listening to you, and they aren't going to listen unless you have their attention.

Since capturing the attention of your audience is the most important function of your introduction, let's consider a few specific techniques:

The rhetorical question. A rhetorical question is one designed to plant an idea for consideration. You might begin by saying:

What are the problems that are of most concern to the adolescents of today?

You would then go on to answer this question in the body of your speech.

The startling statement. This can be an extremely effective attention-getting device. An audience is bound to take some notice of the speaker who begins by saying:

It is almost certain that some time within the next ten years California will experience a major earthquake.

The message
The speaker
The audience

The illustrative anecdote. This device can be used just as effectively in an introduction as in a conclusion. Make sure you tell the story well; be clear and succinct. Write out the first few words to be sure you get off to a good start. Even if you think you know the story well, getting started may be more difficult than you realized.

The humorous anecdote. This technique has some advantages as an opener because it not only gains attention, but it also establishes rapport with the audience. If you can get your audience to laugh, you know they are participating in the communication process, and therefore that they are listening. The added advantage is that when the audience relaxes, you are more likely to relax. Make sure, however, that your joke has a point that relates in some way to the main idea of your speech; then, even if you don't get a laugh, you still have a point. The pitfall, of course, is being corny or trite, but be careful too about telling off-color jokes; they are very likely to backfire with the wrong audience.

These are just a few of the devices you might use. With a little imagination you should be able to come up with a lot more. The important thing is that your introduction be planned. Getting started is going to be one of your biggest obstacles. Regardless of the kind of introduction you decide on, write out the first words on your outline. Be sure you know exactly what you are going to say when you face the audience and open your mouth.

Prepare your bibliography   Your outline should contain a list of the references you have used. For the sake of practice, you should put them down in regular bibliographic form.

Periodicals: Basso, Hamilton, "The Boswell Detective Story." *Life,* vol. 28, pp. 93–104, Dec. 4, 1950.
Books: Clifford, James L:, *Young Sam Johnson,* McGraw-Hill, New York, 1952.

For other kinds of works ask your English teacher or your librarian for the proper bibliographic form.

WRITING YOUR FINAL OUTLINE

There are several things to remember when you draft your outline in final form:

Divide your outline into parts. Your outline should have four parts. the introduction, the purpose statement, the body, and the conclusion. Clearly identify each of the parts, and leave extra space between them.

Number or letter all your headings. Designate your main headings with roman numerals, your subheadings with capital letters, and your specific examples with arabic numerals.

Use the proper form of indention. Indicate each level of subordination by its proper indention, so that the structure is clear at a glance.

The point is that the structure of your outline should clearly display the relationship of each idea. Your instructor shouldn't have to spend his time trying to figure out how your material is organized before he can see what you plan to say—and neither should you.

Look at the following outline for a speech on television lighting. Note the device used in the introductory sentence to pique the curiosity and the way in which the purpose statement provides a reason for the audience to listen. The presummary indicates the areas that will be covered, the main headings are consistent with the presummary, and the support material is relevant to each heading. Note also that the conclusion reinforces the main idea of the speech.

TELEVISION LIGHTING

Introduction

The other day I heard someone say, "Trim the 750 and put a kookie under the skrim."
I was in a television studio and was listening to the lighting technicians.

Purpose statement

Understanding the basic principles of television lighting will enhance your appreciation of television shows.
    A. Types of lights and their uses
    B. Normal lighting procedure
    C. Special-effects lighting

Body

  I. There are two basic kinds of lights used in all television studios, the spotlight and the scoop.
    A. The spotlight

     1. Most versatile and most frequently used
     2. Usually 750 or 1,000 watts, but may be larger or smaller
     3. Several different adjustments
        (a) Can be rotated up, down, or sideways
        (b) Bulb can be moved forward or backward
        (c) Barn doors can be placed in front
        (d) Skrim or a kookie can be placed in front
  B. The scoop
     1. Designed to spread light over a large area
     2. No adjustments
II. Normal lighting situations, such as news or interview shows, are set up in a standard fashion.
  A. Actors in one place
  B. No dramatic effect required
  C. Basic positions for normal lighting
     1. Keylight
     2. Fill light
     3. Backlight
III. Special-effects lighting requires much skill and imagination.
  A. Cameo effect
     1. Light face, dark background
     2. Spot and no fill
  B. Dramatic lighting
     1. Sharp delineation of features, dark shadows
     2. Spot, minimum fill, and no back light
  C. Dynamic lighting
     1. Lights flashing on and off
     2. Timed to music or sound effects
     3. Illusion of thunderstorm

Conclusion

No lighting job is simple; even the routine jobs take much effort.
Lighting can be one of the most creative aspects of television.
Often the difference between a good television show and a mediocre
one depends on the skill of the lighting technician.

No matter how good your material is, you don't have a speech until you
have organized your ideas and information into a single clear message to
present to your audience. This may be the area of speech preparation that
will give you the most difficulty, because it also requires that you organize
your thinking. You may find when you start outlining that your clear idea
of what you want to say is a lot hazier than you thought it was. If your

speech isn't clear enough for you to outline, it won't be clear enough for your audience to follow.

QUESTIONS FOR DISCUSSION

1 How much does the length of a speech affect the attention of the audience? What do you think is the optimum length for an effective speech?

2 Do you find there is some structure in your own conversation? In casual conversation do you ever think ahead to what your next point is going to be? Do you ever try to direct a conversation so that it stays on one central idea?

3 What effect does organization have on communication? Is it possible for a speech to be overorganized? If so, in what way might this affect communication?

4 Can you identify the organizational pattern in this chapter? What is the organizational pattern in the next chapter?

5 What techniques besides those mentioned in the text might be used in an introduction? Is it possible for an attention-getting device to be too dramatic? If so, in what way? What might be the result?

6 What kind of conclusion has been used in the speech on television lighting? Do you think it is effective? Can you think of other ways in which this speech might be concluded?

STUDY GUIDE

I. Outline your material to provide a clear sequence of ideas for yourself as well as your audience.
II. Rewrite your purpose statement and add a presummary that indicates the areas of development you intend to cover.
III. Write main headings for each of your areas of development.
   A. Your main headings should be consistent with your presummary.
   B. Each one should say something significant about your topic.
   C. Your headings should follow a consistent pattern.
      1. The topical pattern breaks the speech into its component parts.
      2. The chronological pattern is useful for explaining a process or discussing a progression.
      3. The spatial pattern organizes material in terms of physical location.

    4. The problem-solution pattern is based on describing a problem and then discussing a solution to it.

    5. The indirect pattern is a progression from the least controversial to the most controversial points of a thesis.

IV. Support and develop your main headings.

    A. All examples must be relevant to the heading that governs them.

    B. The structure of your outline should clearly show the relationship of your ideas.

V. Plan your conclusion to make the most of the audience attention at this point in your speech.

VI. Plan your introduction to orient the audience to your topic and establish its importance, establish rapport with the audience, and capture your audience's attention.

VII. Prepare your bibliography.

VIII. Write your final outline.

CHAPTER 5

The theory of argumentation

Most of the considerations in preparing a speech to inform also apply to the speech to convince. Before we discuss this kind of speech, however, let's take a brief look at some underlying theory. The theory of argumentation is complex, and we will cover just the bare essentials. There is no guarantee that a logically sound argument will change someone's mind. People aren't always logical. However, it is certainly one of the factors in persuasion, and it will be important for you to know whether your arguments are sound or not. It isn't difficult to win an argument, but it is sometimes difficult to know when you have lost.

INDUCTIVE AND DEDUCTIVE REASONING

In his book *The Rhetoric*, Aristotle outlined a distinction between inductive and deductive reasoning. *Inductive reasoning*, sometimes referred to as the "scientific method," begins with a number of examples or observations and proceeds to some conclusion drawn from this evidence. The validity of the conclusion depends on the amount and substance of the evidence that supports it. When Newton formulated the law of gravity after observing falling objects, he was using inductive reasoning. Statistical sampling is also done on this basis. A random sample of people is examined on some point, and from these examples a general conclusion is drawn about the population as a whole. Inductive reasoning proceeds from the specific to the general. *Deductive reasoning* proceeds from the general to the specific. For example, if the general conclusion is that all falling objects follow the law of gravity, we would deduce that some specific object also follows this law.

THE SYLLOGISM

The basis of deductive reasoning is the *categorical syllogism*. A syllogism consists of three statements—the major premise, the minor premise, and the conclusion that follows from them:

All men are mortal.
John is a man.
Therefore John is mortal.

If both premises of a valid syllogism are accepted as true, then, according to the laws of formal logic, the conclusion must necessarily be accepted as true. For the syllogism to be valid, however, the subject of the major premise (all men) must be *distributed*; it can have no exceptions. As soon as you add a qualification of any sort, the syllogism is no longer valid:

Most men pay taxes.
John is a man.
Therefore John pays taxes.

Here the conclusion doesn't follow. To show that John pays taxes we would also have to show that he is one of the "most men" who do.

Now let's look at a slightly trickier problem:

All dogs are animals.
All cats are animals.
Therefore all cats are dogs.

It's obvious that the conclusion is not valid, but why? The form appears to be the same as that of our first example. If you look more closely, however, you will see that in the first example the *subject* of the major premise (men) is the *predicate* of the minor premise (man). This term is called the *middle term*, and its position is the key to a valid syllogism. The middle term must appear, in just this relationship, in both premises. It cannot appear in the conclusion. Moreover, in the conclusion the *minor term* must be the subject and the *major term* the predicate. Otherwise look what can happen:

All dogs are animals.
All cocker spaniels are dogs.
Therefore all animals are cocker spaniels.

The categorical syllogism is the foundation of formal logic, but there are two other types of syllogisms that come up occasionally. The *hypothetical syllogism* has as its major premise a conditional proposition:

If I am a man, then I am mortal.
I am a man.
Therefore I am mortal.

In the *disjunctive syllogism* the major premise contains two alternatives, at least one of which is true:

I am either mortal or immortal.
I am not immortal.
Therefore I am mortal.

Each of these types has its own rules of validity.

In the examples above it is easy to tell whether the syllogism is valid or not. However, invalid syllogisms are not so easy to recognize when they are buried in rhetoric. Look at this example:

Government investigations have fairly well established the fact that the Communist Party has supported the Negro revolution right from the very beginning. There is considerable evidence to show that the Communists have provided both leadership and financial backing. In the violent demonstrations on college campuses all over the country the students have consistently supported the cause of the black revolutionaries. It is plain that the students involved in these demonstrations are inspired by the Communist doctrine.

If you read this carefully you will see that it is actually a syllogism. But is it valid or invalid? Now, be careful. Don't make a judgment based on your own sentiments. Break the syllogism down into its essential parts:

Communists support the Negro revolution.
Student demonstrators support the Negro revolution.
Therefore student demonstrators are Communists.

As you can see, the form here is the same as our example that said all cats are dogs.

This may seem to be a pretty slick way of analyzing arguments, but there are some pitfalls. For example, it is entirely possible for a syllogism to be valid even when the conclusion is untrue. Suppose your father were to tell you this:

> No, son, you can't have the car tonight. I've been doing a lot of reading on the subject of teen-age driving. The insurance reports clearly indicate that most automobile accidents are caused by male drivers between the ages of eighteen and twenty-five. There's no question about it. Young men in that age bracket are bad drivers, and since you are nineteen, that includes you.

Does he have a valid syllogism? As a matter of fact, he does:

> All young men between eighteen and twenty-five are bad drivers.
> You are a young man between eighteen and twenty-five.
> Therefore you are a bad driver.

Does this mean you have to give up and ride the bus? Not at all (provided your father is a reasonable man). You can't attack his logic but you can question the validity of his major premise. He has used a *distributed* term when it should have been *undistributed*. He can't say that *all* young men between eighteen and twenty-five are bad drivers (he can say it, but he can't back it up). All he can say is that *most* of them are bad drivers. Once you get him to change the "all" to "most," which qualifies his major premise, then you can attack his logic.

LOGICAL FALLACIES

The study of formal logic is similar in some respects to the study of mathematics. If a syllogism is properly constructed—that is, if the major and minor premises are both true—then the conclusion follows, and logically it must be accepted. However, mathematics deals with numbers, which have clear and objective meanings. In dealing with words, which can have all kinds of different meanings, the issues are not always so clear cut. Nevertheless, you should learn to recognize fallacies in reasoning so that you know when an argument is logically sound. You can be certain that others will spot the faults in any argument you present, so you had better make sure it will hold up under scrutiny.

Certain logical fallacies have been recognized since the time of the classical rhetoricians, and many of them are still known by their Latin names. All discourse contains some questionable reasoning and you can avoid logical fallacies only in a relative sense. Their offensiveness is primarily a matter of degree. It is important, however, that you understand the concepts.

Insufficient evidence   This is a broad accusation; in any controversial issue there is never sufficient evidence. In fact if all the evidence were available, the issue would probably not be controversial. There are times, however, when the lack of *essential* pieces of evidence can make an argument unacceptable. In such cases you may be charged with speaking in generalities or making unfounded claims—in other words, of making an assertion which you have failed to support.

You hear examples of this kind of fallacy all around you:

> Politics is a dirty business. Nobody in Washington is really honest. They're all looking out for their own special interests. They don't vote for what they think is right; they vote the way lobbyists tell them to. The organization that has the strongest lobby is always going to get its way.

Count the number of unsupported assertions. In all likelihood the speaker would be unable to name a congressman who is dishonest or who does not vote for what he thinks is right, or to name a lobby that always gets its way. You can avoid the charge of insufficient evidence if you make it a point to have at least one example for every assertion you make.

Another aspect of this fallacy relates to attitudes rather than arguments. The person who operates on the basis of stereotypes thinks that he already has all the facts he needs in order to make a judgment. He may never actually make the statement that all fat people are jolly, or all Latins are passionate, or all Irishmen are quick-tempered, or all Communists are treacherous. However, the statements he does make are based on the implicit assumption that these are unquestionable truths.

Unreasonable extrapolation   Extrapolation is an inference that what has started in the past and continues in the present can reasonably be expected to continue into the future. Some amount of extrapolation is a necessary part of our functioning. We infer that the sun will rise tomorrow, since it has come up every morning in the past. However, extrapolation beyond a reasonable point loses its validity. We may be able to predict the total population next year, or even in thirty years—*provided* the rate of growth remains the same. Extrapolation is based on the continuation of a present trend or rate. Hence it is valid only up to the point where we can safely assume that this trend will be unaffected. A business might be safe in planning on the basis of sales figures extrapolated over the next three months, but given all the vagaries of the economy, a prediction of what its sales will be ten years from now would be sheer conjecture.

The non sequitur   The literal meaning of this term is "not in sequence"; in other words, the conclusion does not necessarily follow from what has been stated. There may be a relationship, but too many steps have been left out for there to be a clear connection. For example, you might hear someone say

> Of course we have to fight the war in Vietnam. If we don't our grandchildren will be growing up under communism.

Failure to fight the war in Vietnam could conceivably affect our form of government, but the conclusion is too remote for the assertion to hold without evidence of an actual connection. It is difficult, of course, to avoid every element of the non sequitur without getting hopelessly bogged down in awkward detail, but you should certainly be able to avoid gross violations.

Post hoc, ergo propter hoc   Literally this expression means "after this, therefore because of this." It refers to a particular kind of non sequitur argument. The fact that one event follows another does not necessarily mean that the first one caused the second. Actual cause-and-effect relationships are quite difficult to establish. You have probably noticed, for example, that scientists are very careful to state only that there is a *link* between cigarette smoking and cancer instead of trying to support the claim that smoking *causes* cancer. Nevertheless, people often jump to the unwarranted conclusion that a time relationship indicates a causal relationship. Many people still believe that Herbert Hoover caused the depression because the stock market crashed after he was elected, and even that the stock market rises and falls with the length of women's skirts.

Ignored effects   This kind of fallacy might be referred to as "burning down the barn to get rid of the rats." In many instances a solution may have consequences far more serious than the problem it purports to solve. You have probably heard proposals of this sort:

> The only way to keep communism from spreading is to drop a bomb on Russia.

> Campus riots disrupt the entire educational process; all student demonstrators ought to be put in jail.

The responsible speaker must consider not just his immediate goal, but *all* the consequences of anything he proposes.

The red herring   The origin of this term is uncertain, but it refers to an argument designed to divert attention away from the main issue. A speaker who bases a case for capital punishment on the menace of organized crime is "drawing a red herring across the path." The inverse of this fallacy is sometimes referred to as the "straw-man" argument. The speaker concentrates his attack on a minor objection that can easily be refuted. For example, in advocating fluoridation of the water supply he might spend his time denouncing the contention that fluoridation is a Communist plot so that he can avoid coming to grips with the real objections. A speaker often resorts to this device when he lacks the real evidence to support his thesis.

The circular argument   This is an argument that is used as proof of itself. For example, basing a claim that the Bible is the word of God on statements that are made in the Bible would be a circular argument. One student who was contending that marijuana should not be legalized because it was harmful finally came around to the argument that its harm lay in the possibility of arrest—since it was illegal. The circular argument sounds as if it would be easy to detect, but when it is skillfully concealed in rhetoric it is often difficult to spot.

The distorted example   This is another refinement of the non sequitur. It is the use of an example to "prove" a point that it does not prove. One of the most blatant instances of this fallacy occurred in the early 1940s, when the United States government interred thousands of Japanese-Americans as security risks despite the fact that there had been no indication of their disloyalty. A well-known news columnist stated that since no incident of espionage or sabotage had ever been traced to any Japanese-American, this was proof that they were well organized and merely awaiting a strategic time to strike. As incredible as this assertion was, it was actually widely accepted. The distorted example crops up frequently in the use of statistics. For instance, a speaker may assert that an increase in the number of arrests is evidence of an increase in crime. It is also commonly employed in propaganda campaigns, often with the deliberate purpose of deception.

Begging the question   This is an appeal that an assertion be accepted on some basis other than the evidence. Usually it is used in conjunction with a "hooker" designed to appeal to the listener's emotions or sense of status:

Anyone with political sophistication knows that civil disobedience is a clear danger to society.

We all want to think we are politically sophisticated, and in order to be so, we go along with the assertion. This, of course, saves the speaker the trouble of trying to support it.

Debaters have sometimes been charged with concentrating on argumentation at the expense of truth. Truth is, of course, the prime consideration in the discipline of speech. From a purely practical standpoint, however, the debater learns to avoid faulty reasoning because he knows it will destroy his own case. You will have to test any evidence you present just as the debater does. It is your responsibility both as a speaker and as a listener to be able to distinguish between sound and faulty reasoning.

QUESTIONS FOR DISCUSSION

1 If an argument is valid, is the conclusion necessarily true? Will it necessarily be accepted? Why?

2 Do you believe that an argument is more effective when it is logically sound? Will a true conclusion always prevail, regardless of the argument from which it derives?

3 Do you think that most people recognize fallacies in logic? Would you consider it ethical to use logical fallacies to convince someone of something you sincerely believed in?

4 Can you convince someone he is wrong by pointing out fallacies in his argument? Is it possible to recognize a fallacy and still believe the argument to be true?

5 Do you think that argumentation is the most important factor in persuasion? What other factors are involved?

STUDY GUIDE

I. Inductive reasoning proceeds from the specific to the general conclusion, whereas deductive reasoning proceeds from a general conclusion to a specific application.
II. The basis of deductive reasoning is the categorical syllogism.
  A. A syllogism consists of three statements—the major premise, the minor premise, and the conclusion.

B. The key to a valid syllogism is the position of the middle term.
III. Logical fallacies are often a matter of degree, but you should be able to recognize gross violations.
A. The fallacy of insufficient evidence is an unsupported assertion.
B. Unreasonable extrapolation is an inference beyond the point of probability.
C. A non sequitur is assertion that does not necessarily follow from the stated cause.
D. *Post hoc, ergo propter hoc* is a confusion of temporal sequence with causal sequence.
E. The fallacy of ignored effects refers to a solution with consequences more serious than the problem it purports to solve.
F. The red herring is an argument intended to distract attention from the main issue.
G. The circular argument is an argument used as proof of itself.
H. The distorted example is one used to prove a point that it does not prove.
I. Begging the question is an appeal to accept an assertion on some basis other than the evidence.

CHAPTER **6**

The basis of persuasion

Ever since man began thinking in abstract terms he has been concerned with the nature of truth. Many of the early Greek writers focused their attention on persuasion because they recongized that truth is not self-evident, even to the most intelligent of men. Whatever absolute truth may exist, the only truth we can know is just that—the truth as we know it. In this sense, then, truth is what we believe to be true, and since our beliefs are subject to persuasion, it follows that the truth can become what the most effective persuader makes it.

There is, of course, a fundamental difference between coercion and persuasion. Coercion may have a direct effect on a man's behavior, but it has little effect on his beliefs. There are many areas in which we are motivated by the desire to avoid some unpleasant consequence. However, as soon as the threat of the consequences is removed, the motivation disappears. It is unlikely that everyone would keep on paying taxes if the penalty for not paying them were suddenly revoked. The effects of

The message
The speaker
The audience

persuasion are less direct, but they are more far reaching. A person whose belief has been changed continues to act out of a positive conviction which provides its own motivation.

COGNITIVE DISSONANCE

Persuasion is possible only when one is willing to be persuaded. The law of inertia applies to people as well as other material objects: a body at rest will remain at rest until something happens to disturb the homeostasis. Any state of conflict is less comfortable than a state of harmony or equilibrium. Whenever we are presented with new information that conflicts with our present knowledge or beliefs, this equilibrium is upset and we are in a state of *cognitive dissonance*. Equilibrium is restored by reaching a decision that resolves the conflict.

Some people avoid having their equilibrium upset at all by simply rejecting anything that doesn't fit in with their pattern of thinking. This is the kind of person who might say, "Don't confuse me with the facts; my mind's made up." Most people will consider and evaluate a new idea. However, the extent to which they are willing to accept it depends primarily on the strength and complexity of their present beliefs. Ideas that touch on strong emotional convictions or are intimately tied to a whole set of values and beliefs are very likely to be rejected regardless of the objective evidence.

Regardless of the eventual outcome, all persuasion begins with a state of cognitive dissonance. The speaker presents an idea or a fact that conflicts with the listener's present belief in order to create this state and then offers his solution as a means of resolving it. Even if the solution is rejected, if his arguments are well constructed and strongly supported, the state of dissonance reopens what may have been a closed issue in the listener's mind. If a speaker accomplishes no more than this, he has accomplished a great deal. The effects of persuasion are long range, and the ideas he has planted for consideration may be fed by others and eventually grow. Attitudes and beliefs are formed much the same way as stalagmites, in that each drop of water contributes to the eventual result.

THE MODES OF PROOF

Aristotle contended that persuasion is accomplished by three "modes of proof," which he called *logos, pathos,* and *ethos.* These correspond roughly to the logical proof, the emotional proof, and the character of the speaker.

The logical proof   Logos refers to the facts, the evidence, and the reasoning. Sometimes you will hear a speaker say

> Let's examine the facts of the case.

By focusing attention on the evidence, he hopes to persuade you that his argument is based entirely on reason. Of course, factual evidence can be found to support either side of a controversial issue; otherwise, by definition, the issue would not be controversial. A speaker merely selects that evidence which supports his contention. The information he presents may or may not alter the opinion of the audience. They may reject it as untrue or dismiss it as insignificant. They may also consider it insufficient to prove the point. A speaker who contends that a local government is riddled with corruption would need more than one or two examples to make any impression on an audience that supports this government.

The emotional proof   Clarence Darrow once observed:

> You don't have to give reasons to the jury. Make them want to acquit your client and they'll find their own reasons.

It is easy to say that we should weigh all the evidence before we make a decision, but we never have all the evidence. There are also times when emotional factors must supersede any objective evidence. The plight of a starving child is not subject to objectivity. The very survival of nations has sometimes been determined by response to an emotional appeal. Franklin D. Roosevelt's appeal to the American people in 1933 was more effective than any factual statement he might have made:

> The only thing we have to fear is fear itself.

Appealing to the emotions is a perfectly legitimate means of persuasion as long as the appeal itself is an ethical one.

The character of the speaker   All through history there have been speakers whose words have swayed millions—Churchill, Hitler, Castro, Kennedy, King. The personal magnetism of such speakers is a quality called *charisma*. But were their words really more potent or more eloquent than words of less magnetic speakers? Can the words themselves be separated from the men who spoke them? If someone other than Martin Luther King had said, "I have a dream ... ," would the words have had the same impact? Ethos, the qualities of character projected by a speaker, is perhaps the most illusive of all the Aristotelian modes of proof. If the audience does not see the speaker as a man who is sincere, trustworthy, and knowledgeable, they may reject his evidence, and they will certainly reject any emotional appeal he may make. Aristotle contended in *The Rhetoric* that a speaker established his ethos directly during a speech:[1]

> Persuasion is achieved by the speaker's personal character when the speech is spoken as to make us think him credible. We believe good men more fully and more readily than others: This is true generally whatever the question is and absolutely true where exact certainty is impossible and opinions are divided. This kind of persuasion, like the others should be achieved by what the speaker says, not by what people think of his character before he begins to speak.

Nevertheless, it is apparent that when a speaker has a reputation the audience will be influenced by it. They will frequently decide what to believe and what not to believe on the basis of the speaker's prestige. In general people are more inclined to take the word of someone whose opinion is highly regarded by others and whose expertise has received public recognition in the form of rank or position. Your may disagree with the Secretary of Defense that the antiballistic missile is necessary to preserve the balance of power, but his opinion is more likely to be taken at face value than yours. Yours will have to be supported.

THE RESPONSIBILITIES OF PERSUASION

One speech course may not produce a world-shaking orator. However, it does make a contribution, and frankly, as a human being I am concerned about the way my world gets shaken. Effective persuasion can be a powerful weapon, and it carries the same responsibility as any other weapon.

You may feel that a student speech is not going to influence anyone's opinion, but remember that the views we hold are based entirely on the influences to which we are exposed. Our early years are the most formative, and the strongest influences are our family, teachers, and friends. Later we are influenced by the mass media—the books, newspapers, and magazines we read; the radio and television programs we see and hear. We are also influenced by the society in which we live, by our culture and subcultures and the organizations to which we belong. Some of these influences may be quite small, but each contributes to the total and shapes what follows.

[1] *The Rhetoric and Poetics of Aristotle,* translated by W. Rhys Roberts, Modern Library, New York, 1954.

While you are not quite as impressionable now as you were in your earlier years, you may be going through a stage of your life that is almost as conducive to personality and ideological change. You will not be the same person when you finish college that you were when you began. You will be exposed to more different ideas during these years than at any other time of your life. The very fact that you elected to attend college is an indication that you are willing and able to make some changes based on the new information you receive. Much of it will come from what you read and what you hear in your lecture courses, but some of it will come from fellow students—maybe over a cup of coffee, maybe in your speech class. Each contribution will be small, but each adds to the eventual result.

Occasionally a student speech will have real impact on a nationwide and even a worldwide basis. Certainly the words of Mario Savio, the leader of the Free Speech Movement at the University of California in Berkeley, were heard in all parts of the globe. When Stephanie Mills stated during the Mills college graduation exercises that the most humane thing she could do for future generations was to remain childless, her words had more impact than those of many of the world's leading sociologists. The greatest consequences of persuasion, however, lie in the fact that its effects can be indirect. Even if your speech alone does not change someone's mind, it may prepare the ground for some later change. If you take your speech assignment seriously, you will earnestly try to persuade your audience to the view you are proposing. To whatever extent this persuasion is effective you share in the responsibility for its consequences. A speaker who sets out purposely to persuade must take into consideration the possible consequences of anything he proposes. If he urges fellow students to bring guns on campus, he cannot disclaim all responsibility if someone gets shot.

The extent to which he is responsible depends on his powers of persuasion. The speaker with much prestige, and hence much influence, carries a large burden of responsibility. But any speaker takes on some as soon as he stands up to speak. You never know who is going to believe you and act upon what you say.

Many people are unwilling to accept the responsibilities of persuasion. They may excuse their silence on the grounds that they have nothing to add, or that someone else can say it better, or that what they say would not make any difference anyway. You *should* have something to add, you *should* be able to say it, and it *will* make a difference. You cannot abdicate your responsibility by delegating it to others. In a free society no man has the right to remain silent. Freedom of speech is of no avail unless it is practiced, and just as you share in the responsibility for your influence, so must you share in the responsibility for speaking badly or remaining silent.

QUESTIONS FOR DISCUSSION

1 Do you believe that there is an absolute, or objective, truth? Do you act on absolute truth or on what you believe is true? In what sense can truth become what the most effective persuader makes it?

2 Where would you draw the line between coercion and persuasion? Which do you feel has been a greater influence on your behavior? At what point do threats and promises become instruments of coercion?

3 Which of the three modes of proof do you feel is the greatest factor in persuasion? Under what circumstances might emotional conviction override objective evidence in a decision?

4 What is the basis of charisma? Would you agree that Hitler was a charismatic speaker? If Martin Luther King had spoken the same words at some other point in history, would they have had the same impact?

5 The Roman teacher Quintilian described an orator as "a good man speaking well." How does the concept of a "good man" relate to a speaker's ethos? Is a sincere and ethical person necessarily a more effective speaker?

6 To what extent do you feel that a speaker is responsible for the consequences of his influence? To what extent is a person responsible for the consequences of some casual comment? Do you feel that those who remain silent can disclaim all responsibility for consequences that their silence permitted?

STUDY GUIDE

  I. Coercion has a direct influence on behavior, but persuasion is more effective because it provides its own motivation.
 II. The basis of all persuasion is cognitive dissonance.
    A. A speaker creates a state of dissonance and then presents a solution to resolve it.
    B. The state of dissonance itself opens the door to later acceptance of a speaker's ideas.

III. Aristotle's three "modes of proof" are logos, pathos, and ethos.
   A. Logos is the body of objective proof.
   B. Pathos is an appeal to the emotions.
   C. Ethos is the character a speaker projects to the audience.
      1. A speaker's ability to persuade depends on the audience's respect for him as a person.
      2. A speaker's prestige is a decisive factor in his influence.
IV. The skill of persuasion carries with it a corresponding responsibility.
   A. All beliefs and the actions that arise from them are the result of influence.
   B. To the extent that a speaker's influence is effective, he shares in the responsibility for the consequences.
   C. Just as a speaker is responsible for his influence, so he is responsible for his failure to influence.

CHAPTER 7

The method of argumentation

Now that we have examined the theory and have considered some of the principles involved in a speech to convince, let's give some thought to the development of this kind of speech. Most of the steps for the speech to inform also apply in preparing a speech to convince. However, there are a few important differences that make this kind of speech more difficult and more challenging.

THE THESIS

As in the speech to inform, the first step is to develop a purpose statement or thesis. The same precepts we discussed in Chapter 2 apply here, but there are a few additional factors you will have to consider.

The accuracy of your thesis statement   Be sure your thesis statement accurately expresses your thesis. On any controversial issue the audience has to understand exactly what you are advocating. Don't mislead them by being too sparing with words. For example,

> I believe the social security program should be abolished.

does not tell the audience that what you actually mean is

> I believe that the federal social security program should be put on a voluntary basis instead of being subsidized by the taxpayer.

Remember that the audience will respond to your proposition in terms of what *they* think you are proposing. Sometimes it is wise to explain specifically how your thesis is limited. If you make the assertion that the United States should eliminate the military-assistance program, it might be a good idea to point out that you are not referring to the deployment of military troops, but only to armaments supplied to other countries for use at their own discretion.

It may be necessary in some speeches to define the terms of your proposition. If you are advocating restrictions on the sale of pornography, you had better define what you mean by pornography. In this context it must be considered an abstract term. The *word* "pornography" does not make pornography itself a specific thing that anyone could readily identify as such. Your audience will have to know exactly what it is you think should be restricted. For that matter, you had also better explain what you mean by "restricted." You may find in situations like this that definition of terms takes up a considerable portion of your speech.

The indirect approach   If your topic is a heated one or your audience is extremely opposed to your view, you may do better to approach your thesis indirectly. Instead of bludgeoning them with the flat statement

> Marijuana should be legalized.

you might begin by saying

> Let's examine the justification for the legal restrictions placed on the use of marijuana.

This is sometimes referred to as the *inductive* method of development; you present your evidence first, and then lead your audience to the conclusion you have drawn from it. This doesn't mean that you should mislead them or compromise in any way on your proposal. However, there is an old adage that "A man convinced against his will is of the same opinion still." Your purpose is to bring the audience around to your point of view, and the more easily they can accept your approach, the more receptive they will be to what you have to say.

Loaded language By the same token, there is no point in unnecessarily antagonizing your audience. A charged statement such as

> Higher education in America has become a stupid and meaningless game played by pseudointellectuals.

may turn off your audience before you even have a chance. to explain what you mean. You could have conveyed the same meaning in the more reasonable statement

> Many colleges and universities in America are not providing a curriculum that is relevant to the needs of the students.

Categorical statements The words "all" and "every" should be used sparingly. Unqualified or absolute statements may put you in an embarrassing position, and you will only have to back down later. Claims such as

> All college general-education courses are a waste of time.

> Every violent demonstration in America has been caused by police interference.

are going to be pretty hard to substantiate.

Grinding your own ax One student delivered what could have been an effective speech advocating adoption of the pass-fail system instead of letter grades. However, he began by saying that he had selected the topic because of the low grade he had gotten on his last speech. In putting the issue on this basis, he undermined the soundness of what he was advocating by making it seem to be only a means to his own personal ends.

As you can see, the speech to convince is more difficult than the speech to inform, because there are more ways you can put your foot in your mouth.

THE ARGUMENTS

You're not going to convince an audience to accept your proposition without showing evidence on each issue. In a speech advocating the abolishment of capital punishment, for example, it isn't enough to say:

> We know, of course, that the threat of capital punishment is not a deterrent to murder.

As a matter of fact, there is considerable disagreement over whether it is or is not a deterrent, and you can't just dismiss this issue as one that has been resolved. If you contend that it is not a deterrent you will have to back up your assertion with some evidence. This means that you will have to know when you are making an assertion. Don't expect an audience that disagrees with you to accept your own assumptions.

The other side   We have learned a great deal about the factors involved in public speaking since the days of Aristotle. Probably the most valuable information has come from studies by psychologists and sociologists regarding audience behavior and reaction. In one particularly interesting study it was found that when an audience is well informed, presenting both sides of a controversial issue is more effective in changing their opinion than presenting just one side.[1] When a speaker presents only one side, the audience knows there is another side and will reject his views as biased. Moreover, the audience is aware of the arguments on their own side of the issue, and if the speaker does not discuss them he has no opportunity to refute them.

No matter what the issue, you will have to convince your audience that you have considered *all* the evidence and have good reason for having reached the conclusion you did. Otherwise you're going to have trouble persuading them that your opinion is any more valid than theirs. Look carefully at the reasons they have for their view. Don't look only at the incidental, weak arguments just because they are easy to dismiss. If you are advocating that the city fluoridate the public water supply, you may be able to dismiss as irrational and unsupportable the contention that fluoridation is a communist plot. But what about the contention that fluoride may have unknown effects on the human chemical balance, and the argument that other ways of preventing tooth decay are said to be superior?

Remember that your purpose in introducing the opposing arguments is to refute them. Unless your refutation is effective, you will defeat your purpose. One student who was contending that poverty was a serious problem in the United States introduced some statistics by John Parrish, an expert on economic affairs. Parrish reported that 95 to 98 percent of the population had adequate diets, adequate housing, telephones, television sets, and refrigerators. Instead of refuting this claim with evidence to the contrary, she merely retorted that these figures were "absolutely ridiculous." Then she went right on to her next point, leaving the audience

[1]Carl I. Hovland, Arthur A. Lumsdaine, and Fred D. Sheffield, *Experiments on Mass Communication*, Princeton University Press, Princeton, N.J., 1949.

with only Parrish's evidence—and considerable doubt that poverty was any problem at all.

To win your audience away from the view they hold, you have to be able to see what that view is. Try to look at the issue as they see it, and then ask yourself what arguments and what evidence would convince you otherwise.

The status quo   *Status quo* means the existing conditions—the laws currently in effect, the generally accepted standards of morality, or any other present state or situation. It is always necessary to examine the *status quo* carefully to be sure you are not just "tilting at windmills." If you are arguing for acceptance of something that has already been accepted or attacking an evil that doesn't exist, you not only have no case, but you are betraying your ignorance in the very area in which you are claiming to be informed. One student who was advocating liberal abortion laws was unaware that new legislation had already been passed in his state. He was in fact advocating more liberalization than the new law provided, but since his arguments were in reference to a situation that no longer existed, they were not pertinent.

If you are dealing with a proposition of policy you can provide fairly concrete evidence of the *status quo*. There will be records of the law and its terms, of political statements, or of action that has been taken. It is a simple matter to establish the policy and then attack or support it. On questions of *value*, however, the *status quo* may be more nebulous. For example, if you are contending that the young people today are more politically aware than those of a generation ago, your thesis depends on how effectively you can establish the level of awareness of both generations—and this may be a difficult thing to do.

The need or problem   Whether you are attacking or defending the *status quo* you will have to show the existence of some need or problem. If you are defending it, you must make plain that it needs defending. Sometimes the need is self-evident. If you are contending that capital punishment should be retained, you can assume that the audience is aware of the controversy on this issue and the strong movement to abolish it. In other cases, however, it may not be obvious that there is a problem. One student gave a speech on the need to retain the government—sponsored Head Start program for preschool children in low-income areas. It was an excellent informative speech, but he failed to point out that the program was in any danger of being cancelled.

If you are attacking the *status quo*, you will have to make clear the specific weaknesses, inadequacies, or injustices of the present arrangement. In debate these points are called the *need contentions*. They must be carefully constructed so that they relate explicitly to the solution you are proposing. For example, if you were contending that capital punishment should be abolished, your need contentions might be as follows:

  I. Capital punishment is unnecessary as a deterrent to crime.
    A. No crime increase in states that have abolished it
    B. Fear of apprehension more effective deterrent than severity of punishment
  II. Capital punishment is inequitably applied.
    A. The rich seldom executed
    B. The poor and minority groups usually victims
  III. Innocent people may be executed.
    A. Sacco and Vanzetti
    B. The Rosenbergs

The cause   Once you have determined your need contentions you must carefully analyze the cause of the problem you are describing. In some cases the cause is simple to establish. The problems relating to capital punishment, for example, arise from the fact that capital punishment is legal. Sometimes causes are more difficult to pinpoint. In the controversy over juvenile delinquency, for example, the major issue has been disagreement about the causes. However, unless you clearly indicate the cause of the problem, you won't be able to show that what you are advocating will solve it. One student proposed better educational and recreation facilities to prevent riots. He presented considerable evidence that riots were a serious problem and showed that the FBI had identified a number of the rioters as known communists. If he had been advocating suppression of communist agitation he might have had a strong case, but he had given no indication that inadequate facilities had caused the problem.

Your solution   Research has shown than an audience becomes disturbed if they are presented with a problem without some assurance that it can be solved. People resent being upset, and often their resentment is directed at the speaker as the one who has upset them. If your purpose is to disturb your audience, this is a good way to do it, but don't be surprised if they don't like it.

    Whatever the problem you have described, there is always a basis for some solution. Students have sometimes spoken on the population explosion or the arms race and have concluded that the situation is already beyond any solution—that all we can do is sit back helplessly and await the inevitable. If the problem is actually that serious, there is all the more basis for a solution—because if all is really lost, then there is nothing to lose and everything to gain in at least putting up a struggle.

The solution you present in a speech to convince must be a concrete one. The "blue-sky" solution is merely an evasion of the issue. You may propose to your audience we must learn to love our fellow man, or that we must preserve freedom, but you haven't really given them a specific plan for solving the problem. It isn't hard to get people to accept some abstract virtue. Every movement in history has flown the banner of virtue. Those for the war in Vietnam and those against it both base their stands on the preservation of freedom. The disagreement begins when you get down to specifics. Nevertheless, you are going to have to take a stand on some concrete plan. Your proposal may not be met with unanimous approval, but there are times when you must have the courage of your convictions.

Be sure your solution deals with the problem you have outlined. If your plan doesn't fit your need contentions, your thesis will not hold up regardless of how well you have supported the contentions themselves. Sometimes you will have to modify your need contentions to build a proper case for the solution you are advocating. Several years ago the national debate proposition was that the federal government should provide a minimum guaranteed income for all citizens. After showing strong evidence that poverty was a serious problem in the United States, the debaters pointed out that the reason people were in poverty was that they could not get jobs, and therefore a guaranteed income would eliminate poverty conditions. After several debates, however, it became apparent the plan would not meet the needs. A guaranteed income would not necessarily eliminate poverty because there was no assurance that the money would be used to overcome the poverty conditions. The case would be improved, however, by changing the need contentions so that they supported the solution more strongly. Instead of basing the case on the seriousness of poverty, it was based on the inadequacy of the present welfare system. The debaters showed that it did not provide adequate coverage, that it destroyed the incentive to work, and that it contributed to the breakup of the family unit. They were then able to propose that the guaranteed income be instituted instead because it would overcome these problems.

If the plan does not meet the needs, we say that the case is not *prima facie*—and this leads us to the next step.

CONSTRUCTION OF A PRIMA FACIE CASE

A *prima facie case* is one that has no inherent weaknesses; hence the thesis can be rejected only if one of the major contentions can be proved invalid. In this respect it is similar to a syllogism. Suppose a defense attorney were constructing a prima facie case for his client. His thesis would be that his client is innocent; his arguments would be that his client has alibis for every hour of the day on which the crime was committed. In order to disprove this case the prosecuting attorney would have to discredit one of the alibis and then prove that the crime could have been committed during that particular period of time. Suppose, however, that the client had an alibi for every hour except the one at which the crime was actually committed. The other alibis now have no bearing on the issue; an inherent weakness invalidates the entire case.

Let's see how this principle applies to the construction of a speech. Consider the following thesis:

> Section 605 of the Communications Act should be amended to make wire tapping legal under federal law.

What main contentions would we have to prove for this thesis to be irrefutable? We can use the question-and-answer technique to examine this:

Q. Is there a need?
A. Yes.
Q. What is it?
A. Organized crime.
Q. Will the audience accept that organized crime is a problem?
A. Not necessarily.
Q. Is there evidence to prove that it is a problem?
A. Yes.

This gives us our first main need contention:

I. Organized crime is a serious problem in the United States.
   A. Millions of dollars in lost revenue
   B. Responsible for many small crimes at the local level

The subheadings, of course, would be supported with specific examples, as described in Chapter 3. To proceed:

Q. Why does organized crime continue to flourish?
A. Because we can't get the evidence to convict the racketeers.
Q. Why can't we get it?
A. Because wire tapping is illegal.

Q. Could we get the evidence if wire tapping were legal?
A. Yes.
Q. Are there other ways to get it?
A. Yes, but they are not as effective.

This gives us our second main need contention:

II. The legal use of wire tapping would allow law-enforcement agencies to obtain the necessary evidence for conviction.
  A. Racketeers need telephones to operate
  B. Wire tapping most effective method of obtaining evidence

Let's stop here and examine what we have done so far. Do we have a prima facie case? If the audience could be convinced that these two main contentions were true, would they necessarily have to accept the thesis? The answer is "no." The audience could accept both of them and still have a basis for rejecting the need to legalize wire tapping—infringement on individual liberties. Therefore we need one more main contention before we have a prima facie case:

III. Adequate safeguards could be provided so that the right to privacy would not be abridged.
  A. Use restricted to authorized persons only
  B. Court order required

Now, if we could satisfy the audience that all three of these main contentions were true, we would have a prima facie case, and logically they would have to accept the thesis. It can be refuted, of course, by showing that any one of the main arguments is not valid.

SUPPORTING YOUR ASSERTIONS

In preparing a speech to convince you will have to find evidence to support all the main contentions necessary for acceptance of your thesis. Your can't leave out a necessary contention because you don't find the evidence. Keep looking until you do find it—or else change your thesis.

In Chapter 3 we discussed some of the methods of supporting an assertion. Be sure you understand everything that was said there, and then let's look at some further considerations that apply to a speech to convince.

Quotations   There is nothing wrong with using quotations to support an argument, but if you overwork them the audience may begin to wonder if you have any opinions of your own. Do quote someone else when the reliability of the opinion depends on the source. Your own opinion that criminals do not consider the punishment when they commit a crime won't mean much, but a quotation to this effect from the former warden of San Quentin Penitentiary carries some significance.

As in the speech to inform, the person you quote must be an authority in the field you are discussing. The fact that he is well known may be helpful, but the advertising device of capitalizing on a person's reputation in some other field has no place in serious argumentation. A well-known movie actor might be an authority on the film industry, but that doesn't make him an authority on the use of legalized wire tapping in police investigation. If you were to quote Ralph Hogan, you might have to explain to your audience that he is the former district attorney of the state of New York, but you would have a stronger case.

On a controversial issue, especially if it is a heated one, the fact that someone is a recognized authority may not be enough. The weight the audience gives to his opinion will depend on whether he is an authority that they esteem. Earl Warren is a widely recognized authority on constitutional law, but an audience of the John Birch Society isn't likely to be greatly influenced by his opinion. Be sure you take into consideration how your audience will regard the source you are quoting. Be sure, too, that you consider the biases of your source. It's generally a good idea to state the source of your quotation first, so that your audience has a basis on which to evaluate it.

Definitions We have already discussed the need to define the terms of your proposition. The fact that a term is clear to you doesn't mean that your audience will attach the same meaning to it. They may well agree with what you meant—and disagree violently with what they thought you meant. If the audience doesn't understand your key terms it won't do you much good to claim after your speech, "Oh, but we're talking about the same thing."

Facts and figures You can probably find figures to support almost any assertion; make sure the ones you use are both *valid* and *reliable*. During the 1936 presidential campaign a poll of prospective voters showed that Alf Landon would defeat Franklin D. Roosevelt by a landslide. The outcome, of course, was just the reverse. The *Literary Digest*, which conducted the survey, had selected its sample from the telephone directory and automobile-registration records. However, in 1936, in the depths of the depression, the only people who had telephones and automobiles were those in the high-income brackets, who tended to be Republicans. Thus the results of the survey were not valid because the sample did not represent the entire voting public. Such surveys may also be unreliable, because people don't always end up voting the way they said they were going to.

As with other quotations, the reliance the audience places in your figures will depend in large measure on their regard for the source. The U.S. State Department reports and the official Communist Party records give very different figures for party membership. Both are certainly authoritative sources, but your audience may not view them as equally reliable.

More often it isn't the statistics themselves that are misleading but the conclusions that are drawn from them. Figures that show a rising crime rate may not necessarily indicate an increase in crime; they may merely reflect an increase in arrests. Sometimes they indicate a greater willingness on the part of the public to file complaints. Rape cases, for example, were less likely to be reported in the past than they are now. The records show that more automobile accidents are caused by men than by women. However, this doesn't mean that women are better drivers; it just means that men do most of the driving. Recognizing such fallacies in the use of statistics is not just the responsibility of the audience. It is also the responsibility of the ethical speaker.

Analogy and comparison   A *comparison* shows a similarity or difference between two things of the same kind, whereas an *analogy* shows a parallel between two things that were unrelated to each other. For this reason you can't refute an analogy by simply saying that the two things are different. To show that the parallel does not hold you must show *how* they are different. For example, to refute the statement that the war in Vietnam is as justifiable as the war in Korea, you would have to show specifically how the two situations differ. Let's look at a few more examples. How would you refute them?

Suppose someone proposed that the United States should adopt a program of compulsory health insurance because it is just as important to provide every citizen with good health as with a good education. He might argue that since an educated populace is essential to a strong democracy and many would not go to school unless the law demanded it, we have a compulsory education and free public schools. Since it is just as necessary for the citizens of a democracy to be in good health, we should also provide free medical care.

Here's another. Suppose someone said that the National Conscription Act is unconstitutional because military conscription is slavery. Slavery is defined in the Constitution as "involuntary servitude"—in other words, forcing a man into service when he has not volunteered. Since this is exactly what happens to a man when he is drafted, the Sixteenth Amendment, which outlaws slavery, also outlaws military conscription.

Analogies make argumentation particularly interesting because it takes imagination to create them and analytical insight to refute them. They are also effective, because often it is difficult to focus on the points of difference.

Real and hypothetical examples   You can use either real examples or hypothetical examples to support your arguments. However, real examples provide stronger support. Let's say your assertion is that capital punishment leaves open the possibility that an innocent man may be executed. You might support this assertion with the hypothetical case of someone who is from a low-income minority group and has engaged in political activities that are unpopular with the judge and jury. You could point out that such a person might be tried and convicted for reasons having nothing to do with the crime of which he was accused, and once he had been executed, his sentence could not be repealed. You would have a stronger argument, however, if you cited a case in which this actually happened:

> In 1921 Nicola Sacco and Bartolomeo Vanzetti were accused and convicted of murdering a paymaster in Braintree, Massachusetts. Both men were Italian working-class immigrants who spoke very little English and were unpopular because of their radical political associations. They were executed in 1927 even though someone else had confessed to the crime two years earlier.

Remember that any example you use should be concrete and should contain enough details to establish its credibility. Note that this example includes the first and last names of the people involved, some details about the crime, and some specific dates. This kind of detail helps make the example real for your audience.

Now that you have some idea of the considerations in preparing a speech to convince, look at the following outline for a speech on smog control. Note how the material has been organized, the speaker's main contentions, and the means in which he has supported them. As you go over it, check to see whether he has a prima facie case. If he has, how would you refute it?

SMOG CONTROL

Introduction

On October 26, 1948, the residents of Donora, Pennsylvania, became aware that they were being poisoned.

Donora is not the only city where this has happened, and there will be an increasing number of incidents in coming years.

Thesis statement

As the population increases, as cities grow larger, the smog problem gets increasingly severe, and it's time we did something about it.
  A. Seriousness of problem
  B. Contributing causes
  C. What can be done

Body

I. Polluted air is not just a nuisance, it's a killer.
  A. In Donora, over 5,000 people out of 14,000 ill, 20 died
  B. London, Dec. 5, 1952, hospitals filled with respiratory illnesses, 4,000 deaths
  C. New York, deaths on several occasions
    1. In 1953, 200 deaths
    2. In 1960, 80 deaths
    3. In 1963, 400 deaths
  D. Surgeon-General Dr. Richard Prindle: "It's already happening, deaths are occurring. We're going to have an increasing frequency of episodes."
II. The cause of air pollution is no longer a mystery.
  A. Atmospheric temperature inversion
    1. Warm air rises
    2. Forms lid, preventing pollutants from rising
  B. Smoke from chimneys, power plants, and factories
    1. Tiny pieces of carbon, ash, oil, grease, some light and microscopic, stay in air
    2. Contribute about 10 percent
  C. Invisible but deadly gas, 90 percent
    1. 40 percent from power plants, factories burning sulfur
    2. 50 percent from carbon monoxide from cars and trucks
III. Many solutions have been offered, but few of them are workable.
  A. Air conditioners not effective, take out particles but not poison gases
  B. Los Angeles, dig tunnels and suck air out to desert, would require power of eight Hoover dams
  C. Giant mirrors to heat air and cause it to rise
  D. Legislation against industries
    1. Ban on high-pollution fuels
    2. Ban on public dumps

E. Smog devices on automobiles
   1. Inefficiency of internal-combustion engine
   2. 3.75 million autos in Los Angeles responsible for 12,000 of the 13,000 tons of air pollutants
IV. The only way to solve the problem is to eliminate exhaust from autos and trucks
   A. Pollution control director Louis Fuller: "Serve legal notice that after 1980 no gas-powered cars may operate in the major cities of California."
   B. Solution drastic but necessary
   C. Possible to produce enough steam and electric cars

Conclusion

We know that air pollution is not just a nuisance, it is a killer.

We have the means to solve the problem.

We need only lose our reverence for the internal combustion engine.

QUESTIONS FOR DISCUSSION

1 Is accuracy of wording more critical in a speech to convince than in a speech to inform? Explain.

2 Do you consider it a compromise of principle to use the indirect approach? If a speaker indicates that he has personal interests at stake, do you feel that his argument is less valid?

3 How do you react to strongly worded emotional language? When you use loaded language do you get the reaction you expected, or are you surprised by it? Do you sometimes use loaded language deliberately to get a reaction?

4 If you were undecided on an issue, would you be swayed by a strong and persuasive presentation of one side? If so, would your conviction hold— that is would you actually be persuaded?

5 Do you consider the speech on wire tapping to be a prima facie case? If you were going to refute this case, where would you attack it? Do you find that your ability to refute a case depends on whether or not you agree with the thesis?

6 Do you agree that a real example is more convincing than a logically constructed hypothetical example? Why?

STUDY GUIDE

I. Write your thesis statement.
    A. Be sure it is worded so that the audience understands exactly what you are advocating.
    B. Select an approach that your audience can accept.

II. Familiarize yourself with the arguments of the opposing view.
    A. You are not well informed if you have not considered all the available evidence.
    B. Where an audience is aware of the opposing arguments you will have to refute them effectively.

III. Examine the *status quo* to be certain your arguments are pertinent.

IV. Clearly establish the need or problem and show that your solution will resolve it
    A. Construct your need contentions and outline the causes so that they clearly relate to your solution.
    B. Be sure your plan is concrete and meets the needs as you have outlined them.

V. Determine what main contentions you need for a prima facie case.
    A. A prima facie case is one that has no inherent weaknesses.
    B. As with a valid syllogism, the conclusion can be refuted only by attacking one or more of the main contentions.

VI. Be sure that you have support for all your main contentions.
    A. The weight the audience gives to your examples will depend on their esteem for the source.
    B. The validity of your examples will be subjected to close scrutiny for logical soundness.
    C. Real examples are more effective than hypothetical examples.

CHAPTER 8

Preparing your delivery

Once your speech is prepared, you have finished the hardest part of the job. Now it's time to start thinking about your delivery. There are four ways in which a speech can be delivered:

It can be read from manuscript. Political speakers prefer to give their speeches this way for several reasons. There is less danger of their saying something they hadn't meant to say; the presentation is smooth and formal; and advance copy is available for the press. The disadvantages are that rapport with the audience is poor, and sometimes the audience suspects that the speaker is reading someone else's words.

It can be memorized. This is an excellent method for someone who plans to give the same speech a number of times. Usually the speech will improve each

---

The message
The speaker
The audience

time it is given. The speaker can use exactly the words he had planned with no loss in audience contact. Often, however, the speech sounds memorized, especially the first few times it is given, and again, the audience may wonder whether the words are someone else's. The main difficulty is that the speaker is generally concentrating on the words rather than the ideas, and if he forgets the next word he is lost. Moreover, it is difficult to memorize a speech, especially a long one. The time could be better spent in other forms of speech preparation.

It can be delivered impromptu. An impromptu speech is one that is given with no advance preparation. It takes considerable skill and experience to be able to speak effectively on the spur of the moment. Impromptu speaking can be fun, and it is excellent practice. However, if the speaker has no ideas or information on the topic, it can be a great waste of everybody's time.

It can be delivered extemporaneously. The extemporaneous speech is prepared in advance but is then delivered spontaneously. The speaker may use brief notes to jog his memory, but the notes cover only the ideas and information, not the words in which he will express them. He has carefully planned and organized what he has to say, but he chooses his words as he goes along. Hence he can express himself spontaneously, with occasional reference to his notes to help him move smoothly from one idea to the next.

Extemporaneous speaking is the method on which a speech course usually focuses, because it combines the best features of all the other methods of delivery. It allows the speaker to organize his thoughts and information for the most effective presentation and provides him the same kind of audience contact he would have with an impromptu speech.

THE EXTEMPORANEOUS SPEECH

It's a good idea to prepare note cards in addition to your outline. Your instructor will probably want to have the outline while you are giving your speech. From your own standpoint, however, cards are a lot easier to handle while you are speaking. They can be held inconspicuously in one hand; you don't have to put them down if you want to move around or gesture to your audience. You can hold them up to look at without blocking your view of the audience or having to look down and away from them. And cards won't rattle the way a sheet of paper does if your hand just happens to shake a bit.

Your cards can be 3 X 5, or 4 X 6, or 5 X 8—whatever size is most

(1)

Oct. 26, 1948, residents of Donora, Pa., being poisoned

As population increases, cities grow larger, problem becomes more severe

Seriousness   Causes   What can be done

I.   *Polluted air not just nuisance; killer*

    A.   Donora: over 5,000 out of 14,000 ill, 20 died

    B.   Dec. 5, 1952, London: hospitals filled, 4,000 died

    C.   New York: 200 in 1953, 80 in 1960, 400 in 1963

    D.   *Richard Prindle:* "It's already happening--deaths are occurring. We're going to have an increasing frequency of episodes."

---

(2)

II. *Cause of air pollution no longer a mystery*

    A.   Atmospheric temperature inversion; warm air forms lid on pollutants

    B.   Smoke from chimneys, power plants, factories, carbon, ash, oil, grease only 10%

    C.   Invisible but deadly gases 90%: power plants, factories 40%; cars and trucks 50%

The message
The speaker
The audience   **75**

(3)

III. *Many solutions offered, few workable*

    A.   Air conditioners

    B.   Tunnels in L.A.: would need 8 Hoover dams

    C.   Giant mirrors

    D.   Legislation: ban on high-pollutant fuels, close dumps

    E.   Smog devices: 3.75 million autos in L.A. produce 12,000 of the 13,000 tons

---

(4)

IV. *Eliminate exhaust from cars and trucks*

    A.   *Louis Fuller:* "No gas engines in cities of California."

    B.   Solution drastic but necessary

    C.   Electric and steam cars

Conclusion

Air pollution not just a nuisance; a killer
We have means to solve problem
Need only lose reverence for internal-combustion engine

comfortable for you. Here are a few rules regarding their preparation:

Type or write legibly. The print should be dark enough so that you will be able to see it clearly at a glance.

Underline important ideas. Also, put quotation marks around direct quotations, and always include some note on the source of a quotation.

Write on only one side of the card. Don't use both sides. If you have to turn a card over, you may forget whether or not you have already covered the material on the other side. Remember that you are likely to be under some pressure when you are giving your speech.

Don't write a complete transcript of your speech on the note cards. If you do, you will be strongly tempted to read it, and your audience contact will suffer. You won't get the experience you need in extemporizing, and you will probably also get a low grade on your speech. Put on the cards only key words and phrases to serve as reminders of your ideas. If you were giving the speech on smog control that we outlined earlier, your note cards might include the information shown on the preceding pages.

THE IMPROMPTU SPEECH

In case your instructor assigns an impromptu speech as an exercise, you should know something about it. Very little has been written on how to give an impromptu speech. Most writers merely advise you not to let yourself get caught in a situation where you have to give one. In one sense this isn't bad advice. If you can anticipate being called on to speak, even by a few minutes, you can begin organizing your thoughts. If you are a reasonably well-organized person, if you know what you believe and why you believe it, if you have expressed your beliefs in conversation with your friends, the chances are that you will have little difficulty in expressing the same ideas to a group of people.

The only kind of impromptu speech that makes any sense is one on a topic you know something about. There is no point in making your audience sit there and listen to meaningless noises just because you feel compelled to use up the time. There are occasions when a courteous decline is preferable to a gallant attempt.

The best way to prepare for impromptu speaking is to keep yourself well informed on important current topics and get used to discussing them with your friends. Conversation is a good way of testing your ideas and practicing clear, well-organized verbal expression.

Pay attention. Whenever you attend a meeting or gathering of any kind, stay alert and pay attention to what is being said. Think in terms of how you would respond if you were asked to comment on something the speaker had just said.

Give a direct response. Often the impromptu speech will be a response to some question. Begin by answering the question as directly as you can; then qualify and develop your answer. Don't leave your audience wondering what your position is, so that they have to ask the question the second time.

Keep it short. No one expects a full-length speech on the spur of the moment. If the chairman had wanted you to give a major address, he would have included you on the program. Keep your remarks short and to the point. Don't go off on a tangent. Keep the central idea in mind the whole time you are talking, and don't deviate from it.

Keep the end in sight. The hardest thing about an impromptu speech is ending it. Remember that all speeches must have conclusions, whether they are prepared or not. To be sure your impromptu speech doesn't just wither away and trail off into silence, plan your concluding statement as soon as you start talking. It should be something similar to your opening statement. Anticipate your last sentence before you come to it, so you will be able to finish up in a strong, dynamic tone.

Impromptu speaking is not easy. The people who do it well are the ones who do it often and have a large fund of ideas and information to draw on. In this respect good impromptu speeches are not impromptu at all. They reflect ideas that have been given considerable thought and have probably been expressed before in an unstructured situation of informal discourse. When Daniel Webster rose to answer Robert Young Hayne on the Senate floor, someone asked him afterward how he had been able to deliver such an eloquent speech with no preparation; he replied, "I've been preparing that speech all my life."

THE DEMONSTRATION SPEECH

The demonstration speech is often used as an "ice breaker" in speech classes. It is easier to prepare than other speeches, because you can usually pick a subject you know something about, and it requires little research. It is also easier to give, because you don't have to just stand there and talk; having something to do gives you a chance to release the nervous energy that causes stage fright.

There are a number of kinds of materials or "props" that can be used in a demonstration speech.

Speeches with two-dimensional visual aids   Charts, pictures, or maps are usually readily available; if not, they are easy to make. When they are used effectively they can be a big help in explaining your point. If they aren't used properly, however, they can just get in your way. There are some specific points to bear in mind in preparing your displays:

Be sure they are large enough to be seen. Calculate the size and position of your audience and prepare your chart or map so that the person in the farthest corner of the room can see it. This is just as important as speaking loudly enough to be heard.

Keep them simple. A display that is too "busy" will distract your audience. If they can't immediately grasp everything that is on it, they may spend their time trying to decipher it instead of listening to you. Explain everything that needs to be explained and clearly point out how the information you are showing supports what you are saying. Try to avoid including anything on your display that isn't covered in your speech.

Be sure they are neat. The visual aids that you use become a part of your speech. They say something about your attitude toward the audience. Carelessly prepared material indicates that you didn't consider the matter important enough to go to any great bother. In that case, your audience may take the same attitude.

Whatever visual aids you use, be sure you know exactly how you are going to use them. Otherwise you may find yourself tripping over your own material. Figure out where you are going to put your display, how you are going to get it there, and where you are going to stand when you refer to it. Plan when you are going to display your material and how long you are going to leave it up. Here are some tips:

Place your display high enough and in a position where it can be seen. Generally classrooms have hooks and clips to hang things on, but you may have to bring an easel. Position the display so that you can stand to one side of it, without blocking the view of anyone in the audience. This may take some thought.

If possible, don't display your material until you are ready to discuss it. It may be distracting if you put it up too soon. When you rehearse your speech, practice setting your material up while you are talking. It will take some practice to be able to do this quickly and smoothly, but you don't want to leave your audience in silence for any longer than you have to.

Plan how and when you are going to take your material down. If you feel that your display may distract the audience after you have moved on to your next point, take it down at some convenient time. Sometimes, however, it is a good idea to leave it up in case your audience wants to refer back to it later.

Speeches with three-dimensional aids The possibilities here are limited only by your imagination. There may be some restrictions, however, on what you can bring into the classroom. For example, firearms are generally prohibited unless the bolt or firing pin has been removed. Don't bring in any article that is illegal, no matter what you plan to say about it. Animals may or may not be acceptable, depending on the inclination of your instructor, but a word of caution—they are quite unpredictable and may wind up stealing the show.

The same considerations apply as for two-dimensional aids, with a few further ones:

Make sure the demonstration works. When you practice your speech, include the demonstration in your rehearsal. If you are going to show the audience how safety bindings work on skiis, be sure yours work the way they are supposed to. It's embarrassing to start out with a big buildup and then have your demonstration misfire.

Pass objects around only when necessary. Sometimes it is advantageous to pass around something that is too small for everyone to see. Be sure to explain what it is first. However, don't pass around any more things than you have to, and don't have too many objects in circulation at the same time. Whoever is looking at the object is probably not paying attention to you at the moment. If you have a lot of things in circulation, you may lose a good portion of your audience.

Speeches with bodily performance Sometimes your own activity may be the demonstration. Some unusual speeches of this sort have been given. One student crushed grapes in her bare feet while she discussed wine making. Another gave his speech by radio while he was flying 2,000 feet above the campus. Another prepared *hors d'oeuvres* for the entire class in eight minutes. The important thing, of course, is not the uniqueness of your approach, but how good your speech is.

For some speeches you may want to use members of the audience. One student supplied squirtguns filled with different-colored paints to several members of the audience and had them take random shots at a piece of canvas to illustrate a possible new artform. If you plan to use participants from the audience, it's a good idea to line them up in advance. If you spring something on your audience with no warning, you may not get any volunteers, and if you have to pick "volunteers," they may be too embarrassed to participate with any enthusiasm. There are also speeches in which the entire audience may be asked to take part. Some speakers have had the audience join them in yoga exercises, or analyze the lines in the palms of their hands. This type of speech has the advantage of getting everyone actively involved in the communication process, but you have to be careful that your audience doesn't get too carried away.

Remember that the success of your demonstration will depend to a large extent on the quality of your end product. If you are showing how pottery is made on a potter's wheel, you should have something fairly impressive to show your audience when you finish. The impact of your speech is weakened if you have to apologize for an object you produced. Incidentally, you will find it very difficult to perform a complicated operation and talk to an audience at the same time, and if the performance takes a great deal of energy, you may find yourself panting for breath while you are trying to speak. You had better check to be sure you can carry it off. If you can't, pick another topic.

Whatever type of demonstration you use, don't forget that you are in a speech class. Your demonstration is an aid to your speech, not a substitute for it. No matter how skilled you may be in the area you are demonstrating, what you will be judged on here is your skill in speech making.

Speeches with audiovisual aids   You may sometimes have access to audiovisual equipment. Not all speeches are improved by the use of audiovisual aids. If you do decide to use them be sure you are thoroughly checked out on the equipment before you give your speech.

The slide projector. This can be a good aid if you have good pictures. Don't show too many—and have something to say about each one. The disadvantage is that you will not be able to maintain good contact with your audience in a dark room.

The overhead projector. This is one of the most effective of the audiovisual aids. The room doesn't have to be dark for clear projection, and you can face your audience while you use it. However, you will have to obtain your own transparencies.

The opaque projector. With this machine you can show pictures in books and magazines, and even flat objects such as coins. It has two big disadvantages —often the machine is noisy in operation, and the room must be quite dark for effective projection.

The phonograph. If you want to use selections from phonograph records, go ahead and do so. But remember that you will have trouble finding just the right spot to put the needle down, especially if your hand is shaking a bit.

The tape recorder. If you are planning to use music, speech, or sound effects, a tape recorder is easier to use than a phonograph. It can be stopped and started more smoothly, and the right spot on the tape can be found with greater ease.

The motion-picture projector. Film can be worked into a speech just as slides can. The disadvantage is the same as with the slide projector—the room must be dark, and contact with the audience is at a minimum.

Remember that verbal communication is only one of the ways in which people receive messages. Your objective as a speaker is to communicate a message to your audience, and the more ways of communicating you can incorporate in your speech, the more effective your communication will be. If you can augment your spoken message by effective appeals to the visual and other senses, it is certainly to your advantage to do so.

QUESTIONS FOR DISCUSSION

1 Do you feel that a speech that is read or memorized sounds sincere? On what do you base your impression? If a speaker refreshes his memory by referring to his notes, does this affect your impression of his sincerity?

2 In recent years the emphasis has shifted from read and memorized speeches to extemporaneous speeches. What changes in attitude do you think might be responsible for this shift? What sociological changes might account for a tendency toward shorter speeches?

The message
The speaker
The audience

3 Can a demonstration speech be persuasive? What kinds of visual aids might a speaker use for the sake of persuasion?

4 Are there some speeches in which visual aids or demonstrations would be a disadvantage? Are there any speeches that could not be given at all without such aids?

5 What is the advantage of getting an audience actively involved in the speech?

STUDY GUIDE

  I. A speech may be read from manuscript, memorized, delivered impromptu, or delivered extemporaneously.
 II. An extemporaneous speech is delivered from notes.
III. An impromptu speech requires general knowledge of the subject and alert thinking.
 IV. A demonstration speech is often used as an ice breaker.
   A. Two-dimensional aids are effective only when their use is properly planned.
   B. In using three-dimensional aids be sure your demonstration works, that any finished product is effective, and that circulated objects do not divert attention from your speech.
   C. Speeches with bodily performance offer opportunities for audience participation.
     1. Line up audience participants in advance.
     2. Be careful that the audience doesn't get carried away.
   D. In considering audiovisual aids weigh the advantages and disadvantages carefully.
     1. Be sure you are checked out on the equipment.
     2. Evaluate the extent to which conditions of use may interfere with audience contact.

CHAPTER 9

Practicing your delivery

You may spend many hours researching material and preparing your outline, and then produce only a mediocre speech because you have failed to take the easiest step of all—practicing your delivery. Perhaps you feel that rehearsing a speech will change your presentation from honest communication into a "performance" or an "acting situation." A good speech should be natural, and an honest reflection of your personality. However, remember that public speaking is structured, and the goal of structured communication is to convey the greatest amount of information in the shortest time. You don't do your audience any favor by taking up their time with dull, long-winded discourse, and they probably won't listen to you if you do. For that matter, practice in structured speaking will stand you in good stead in unstructured, informal discourse as well. The more clearly and succinctly you can say what you have to say, without a lot of irrelevant side-tracking, the more people in any situation are going to listen to you with interest.

FACING YOUR AUDIENCE

This probably isn't the first time you have spoken in a classroom, but it may be the first time you have formally addressed an audience. Let's start with the fundamentals.

Learning to stand　There will certainly be occasions when you can speak to a group while you are seated, or even perched on the edge of a desk. First, however, you had better learn how to stand—on both feet. Standing with your weight on one foot is no great crime. The problem is that you then tend to shift to the other one, and you are likely to end up rocking back and forth without being aware of it. Your audience will be aware of it. With a firm foundation you are less likely to distract either yourself or your audience with awkward poses.

Avoid the temptation to lean on things. Tables, chairs, and lecterns, are not crutches. To speak effectively you should display a certain amount of physical vitality, and leaning on the furniture gives the impression that you just can't summon up the necessary energy.

Learning to move　Once you get set behind the lectern or the desk, don't feel that you have taken root there. Feel free to move around as long as the movement has some purpose. Don't pace the floor just to dissipate energy, but do move when there is a reason to do so. You may want to walk to the chalkboard to write something down, or turn once in a while to face a part of the audience that can't see you too well.

One particular reason for moving is to close the distance between you and your audience in order to emphasize an important point. It has long been known that the effectiveness of communication varies with the distance between the speaker and the audience. As the distance is decreased, a greater impression of intimacy is created. You may have noticed this effect when a speaker steps out from behind the lectern and moves toward the audience.

Just as you needn't feel glued to one spot, don't feel that your elbows are glued to your ribs. If you can, rehearse your speech in front of a mirror. Experiment with different kinds of gestures to see how they look. Don't plan them for specific points in the speech; if you bring them in on cue, that's exactly how they will look. The important thing is to overcome the reluctance you may have to use gestures at all.

The message
The speaker
The audience

Use your speech class as a laboratory to investigate the effects of various positions and movements. See for yourself what kinds of results you get.

Maintaining eye contact with your audience　The importance of eye contact as a specific factor was established in a study by John Wills in 1961.[1] He found that speakers who were rated as "sincere" looked at the audience an average of 63.4 percent of the time, while those who were rated as "insincere" maintained eye contact only 20.8 percent of the time.

You will hear all kinds of advice about how to maintain good eye contact, but the only way it can really be done is to look people in the eye. When you are facing your audience look directly at each person; as soon as the person you are looking at returns your glance, move on to the next one. Don't focus over the tops of people's heads or stare off into space. The audience may admire your firm jawline, but your faraway gaze won't make them feel that you are really in touch with them. Above all, don't fix your eyes on your notes or on the lectern. Remember, you are talking to people, not just projecting your voice into the room.

USING YOUR VOICE

Now that you have some idea of the factors involved in facing your audience, what happens when you open your mouth to speak? Here, too, there are some points you will have to take into consideration in a structured, public-speaking situation.

Volume　One of the things you are going to have to get used to is that public speaking requires more volume. At first you may feel that you are shouting, but if the instructor tells you to speak up, don't feel inhibited about doing it. He isn't trying to turn you into an extrovert; he just wants to make sure that everyone in the room can hear you. You may be mumbling because you aren't really sure of your material, and you are afraid someone might hear you. If so, go back and review the other steps in speech preparation.

Pitch　Pitch problems can be difficult to overcome, but the first step is to identify them. There are two basic kinds—the *monotone* and the *patterned*

[1] John Wills, "An Empirical Study of the Behavioral Characteristics of Sincere and Insincere Speakers," doctoral dissertation, University of Southern California, Los Angeles, 1961.

pitch. The monotone speaker, sometimes labeled "Johnny one-note," is wearing to listen to, like the same key sounded over and over on a piano. As a result, it becomes difficult to concentrate on what he is saying even when his material is good. If you have this kind of pitch problem, try rehearsing your speech with a tape recorder, and practice varying your pitch. This is often easier to do if you increase your volume, your rate of delivery, and your general level of enthusiasm.

A speaker with patterned pitch has what is known as a "sing-song voice." His voice goes up or down at regular intervals, and the audience tends to concentrate on the pattern rather than on what he is saying. Often this problem is a result of having memorized the speech. Again, a tape recorder is helpful for identifying the pattern and practicing to overcome it.

Vocal emphasis Vocal emphasis is important for the sake of oratory, but it is often essential to clarify your meaning. Look at this sentence:

I didn't say he stole my book.

It contains seven words in the English language, and since we know the meaning of all the words, we might say we know the meaning of the sentence, right? Well, take another look at it. It has seven different meanings, depending on which word you emphasize. Try it. Repeat the sentence to yourself, emphasizing each of the words in order. This is just one more of the many ways you might be misunderstood, when you thought what you were saying was perfectly clear.

When you just said this sentence to yourself, you probably said the emphasized word a little louder and at a slightly higher pitch than the other words in the sentence. You may also have paused slightly just before the emphasized word. In general, vocal emphasis entails some kind of vocal change to set off what you are emphasizing from the surrounding material.

Rate of delivery People can listen faster than you can talk, and if they are left for long without something to listen to, their attention will wander. You will probably have to speak faster than you usually do in casual conversation. There is no one rate of delivery that is best for all speakers, but you should talk as fast as you can without stumbling over words or slurring syllables. For some of you this will be about 90 words a minute, and for others it may be as high as 225 words a minute. Remember, however, that the rate itself is not as important as your clarity; every word and every syllable must be understood.

SPEAKING TO YOUR AUDIENCE

When you deliver your speech you will have to consider how you are going to move from one idea to the next. Your speech should have continuity and should flow smoothly from beginning to end. However, the need for transitions is not just an artistic one. Although you know in your own mind how what you are saying relates logically to your last point, the relationship may not be so clear to your audience. They are more likely to grasp what you are saying if they can see how your information fits into place, instead of having to stop and figure it out for themselves.

There are two kinds of transitions you can employ—*rhetorical transitions* and *vocal transitions*.

The rhetorical transition   This is a sentence or phrase that links what was said before with that which is to come. There are a number of perfectly acceptable stock transitions:

> And so we can see that . . .
> Now let's take a look at . . .
> By the same token . . .
> In the final analysis . . .

Such transitional phrases clearly indicate the organization of main ideas and their relationship to each other. They point out at each stage the direction the speaker is now going to take. The stock phrases will do if your only concern is flawless organization, but your speech will be more interesting if you vary the formula a bit. You don't have to include rhetorical transitions in your outline, but if you do, put them in parentheses.

The vocal transition   One advantage the speaker has over the writer is that he can use vocal transitions to indicate a "shift in gears." There isn't any rigid formula for making vocal transitions; this is a technique that will have to be developed with experimentation and practice. Generally, however, the vocal transition is effected chiefly through a change in volume and pitch. Usually a speaker will drop his voice at the end of one idea, pause slightly, and then begin the next statement at a higher volume and pitch. Often the vocal transition is used in conjunction with the rhetorical transition.

For your vocal transitions to be effective, you will have to think ahead of what you are saying. When you come to the last sentence in a discussion, and especially the last sentence in your speech, you must anticipate it far enough in advance to give yourself a chance to drop down to the period. If you get caught short, you are likely to leave the audience hanging in midair by ending your speech on an upward inflection. This, of course, is what makes extemporizing difficult. You must keep track not only of what you are saying, but of what you have just said as well as what you are going to say next.

Diction   Always use the best diction you possibly can. Nothing will mark you more quickly as immature than the use of immature language—words such as "swell," "guy," "stuff." The use of contemporary vernacular can sometimes be an effective means of establishing rapport with our audience, but like anything else in your speech, it should be used selectively. You may not want your audience to consider you stuffy, but neither do you want them to think you are incapable of expressing yourself in standard English.

THE IMAGE YOU PROJECT

Now that you have some ideas about how to put your speech across let's give some thought to the factors involved in putting yourself across. The message your audience receives and their willingness to accept it is going to be determined in large measure by their perception of you as a person —by your ethos. To be an effective speaker you must not only possess the qualities that will win their respect, you must also project them. The characteristics of ethos are elusive, but there are some fundamental points on which the audience will base their judgment.

Sincerity   This is the primary basis on which an audience will judge your integrity as a speaker. It would be convenient if sincerity were self-evident, if we could always tell the "good guys" from the "bad guys." Unfortunately sincerity and someone else's belief in that sincerity are two different things. You have probably heard people say that they can always tell when a speaker really believes in what he is saying, or that an audience can always detect any trace of insincerity. Nevertheless, the evidence tells us something quite different.

In 1953 Richard Hildreth conducted a study of people's ability to distinguish between sincere and insincere speakers.[2] He had several speakers in a community select their own topics from a list of controversial issues and prepare speeches advocating their own stands on these issues; the speeches were given before an audience and filmed. Each of the speakers was then requested to prepare a speech advocating the

[2]Richard A. Hildreth, "An Experimental Study of Audiences' Ability to Distinguish between Sincere and Insincere Speeches," doctoral dissertation, University of Southern California, Los Angeles, 1953.

opposite side of the same issue; these speeches were also filmed. Thus Hildreth had a set of "sincere" speeches and a set of "insincere" speeches, rated according to the actual convictions of the speakers. He showed these films to a number of audiences and asked them to pick the speakers they considered to be sincere. The results showed that the audiences were unable to make any accurate distinction between speakers who were sincere and those who were not.

Hildreth's results also showed, however, that people *thought* they could perceive sincerity accurately. They had included in their replies the particular characteristics on which they had based their judgment of the speaker's sincerity. In 1961 John Wills studied Hildreth's findings and compiled a list of twenty-three specific traits that the respondents regarded as evidence of sincerity.[3] These traits—which had been displayed by the sincere and insincere speakers alike—included such techniques as maintaining relaxed but erect posture, using conventional gestures, reflecting a pleasant mood, and looking at the audience most of the time. Thus what the audience perceives as sincerity bears little relation to a speaker's actual sincerity; their judgment is in fact based on rather trivial techniques.

It should be clear by now that just being sincere isn't going to be enough. You can't assume that your feeling of sincerity will magically transmit itself to the audience with no effort on your part, and that the techniques of projecting sincerity are needed only by the insincere. Regardless of your own convictions, you may find that you are projecting quite a different image to your audience. This kind of situation frequently arises when you are concentrating on the words of your speech rather than the ideas. You may use expressions that stand out from your usual way of speaking. The audience is aware of the discrepancy and is likely to attribute the artificiality to phoniness. One way to avoid this situation is to practice extemporizing rather than memorizing.

Affability Another major factor in the audience's evaluation of what you say is how well they like you. Think back over your own experience. Haven't you ever rejected what someone said just because you didn't like him, or taken someone's advice because he was your best friend?

In one study with young children, five popular and five unpopular children were picked to perform simple tasks in front of the class. The five popular ones were taken aside and told privately that when their instructions were announced they were to do exactly the opposite of whatever they were instructed to do. The tasks were then announced and per-

[3]Wills, *op. cit.*

formed according to plan, and the children who were watching were told to write down the names of the children who had performed correctly. You guessed it. They named the five children they liked. In case you think this phenomenon is restricted to children, in another study a group of teachers were asked to list the children they liked and those they disliked; then a number of spelling tests that they had already graded were examined. It was found that the teachers had overlooked a significant number of spelling errors on the pages of those they liked.

You may not be happy with the idea that people will accept or reject what you say on the basis of whether they like you or not, but often it happens that way. The rapport you establish with your audience in the first few minutes of your speech may well determine its success.

It is easy to fall back on the easy out that your responsibility is to give a good speech, and if the audience doesn't accept it, that's their problem. If you do, you are missing the whole point of a speech course. Your purpose is not just to speak, it is to communicate. If you aren't communicating with your audience, that's your problem. As a speaker you are part of every speech you give, and it is up to you to develop the individual style that will make you as effective as your words.

QUESTIONS FOR DISCUSSION

1 Do you feel that rehearsing a speech makes it a performance? In what way does rehearsing a speech make the presentation more succinct? Can a speech be overrehearsed? What might the effects be of overrehearsal?

2 Why do people generally stand when they make a speech? Can a seated speaker achieve the same effect? Explain. Why should a speaker include some movement in his presentation? What effect does movement have on attention?

3 What effect does the use of slang have in a speech? Can you cite examples of people who use slang effectively? What is the effect of excessive formality? Which would you say was more detrimental in a speech?

4 Do you believe that people are more likely to accept the ideas of someone who expresses them well? Is it harder for you to reject the views of a good speaker? Would you be willing to accept the support of someone who accepted your views because he liked your style?

5 Why is sincerity a key factor in persuasion? Would it be possible for an

audience to accept an idea that they felt the speaker didn't believe in himself?

6 Do you feel that it is necessary to like someone in order to accept his ideas? Could you support a cause that was also supported by someone you thoroughly disliked and distrusted?

STUDY GUIDE

I. Learn to stand and move in front of your audience.
  A. Rest your weight on both feet to avoid awkward and distracting poses.
  B. Practice moving around and gesturing when you rehearse your speech.
    1. Approaching the audience gives an effect of greater intimacy.
    2. Experiment with different kinds of gestures.
  C. Maintain eye contact with your audience by looking directly at each person in turn.
II. Learn to use your voice effectively.
  A. Don't feel self-conscious about increasing your volume.
  B. Watch for pitch problems.
  C. Practice vocal emphasis for clarification of meaning.
  D. Adjust your rate of delivery.
III. Consider transitions and diction.
  A. Incorporate transitional phrases in your wording.
  B. Practice vocal transitions in moving from one idea to the next.
    1. A drop in pitch usually signifies the end of a sentence or idea.
    2. Anticipate pitch changes far enough ahead to give yourself time to make them.
  C. Select your diction carefully.
IV. Consider the image you project to the audience.
  A. An audience's perception of your sincerity will depend not on your actual convictions, but on the sincerity you project to them.
  B. An audience will usually accept or reject what you say on the basis of how well they like you.

CHAPTER 10

Analyzing your audience

By this time you have probably made several speeches, and maybe you have noticed that some were well received and others were merely tolerated. In Chapter 2 we discussed some general attributes of a typical college audience, and perhaps you took them into consideration when you prepared your speeches. However, this isn't the only kind of audience with whom you will ever have to communicate. Most of the people to whom you will be speaking later will not be college undergraduates. Many will not be as tolerant of new ideas, or as interested in encouraging you; some may be downright hostile and antagonistic. You won't be in the protected environment of the classroom, where your instructor serves as a stimulus to see that your audience pays attention and can bail you out if the question period gets out of hand. You will be on your own, and it's a good idea to be ready for it.

The message
The speaker
The audience

Suppose you have been invited by one of the local service clubs to speak at their weekly luncheon meeting. Let's hope that by now you have acquired enough confidence from your speech class to accept. That's the first step. Now what? Find out as much as you can from the person who asked you to speak. You'll want to know the size of the group, and whether this is a formal or an informal occasion. If the group is large and the occasion is a rather formal one, you may need a public-address system. Be sure to find out how long a speech you are expected to give and whether there will be a question period afterward. You should also know whether there are other speakers on the program, and if so, what their topics are. If you plan to use visual aids, you had better find out what facilities are available. You may need an easel for charts, a chalkboard, a projector and screen, or a pointer. These aren't usually provided unless you request them.

The most important consideration, however, is that your speech itself meet the needs and expectations of the audience. Find out why you have been asked to speak. Were you picked because your audience wants information on a particular topic? Or do they want you in particular as the speaker, regardless of your topic? (This is not uncommon if you have established a reputation.) Is this a group that prefers to steer clear of controversial issues, or do they want to hear your views on an issue of interest to them? It is not courteous to take advantage of a speaking situation to push some pet cause unless you have been specifically invited to do so. If you are asked to give an informative speech, be sure that you do just that. Take another look at the discussion of speech purposes in Chapter 2.

Before you even begin preparing your speech you will have to give thought to the audience you are going to address. In order to communicate with them effectively there are a number of factors you are going to have to take into consideration.

WILL THE AUDIENCE BE INTERESTED?

Let's say that you have been asked to give an expository speech on the local community college because this is an area in which you are informed. Your topic has been specified, but it's still a pretty broad one. In organizing your material you will have to focus on the points that are most relevant to the people you are talking to—and to do this you have to know something about them.

Suppose, for instance, that the club has invited a group of high school students to hear you. In this case you might orient your remarks to those who were considering enrollment. You could talk about the curriculum and the courses that are offered, or about social activities and athletics —in short, the aspects that would be in interest to incoming students. What if you were addressing the businessmen of the community, the ones who pay the taxes that support the college? Here your approach would be slightly different. You might discuss the financing of the college and point out what the taxpayer is getting for his money—say, the cultural activities the college provides for the community. If your audience were made up of prospective teachers planning their careers, you could discuss some aspects of teaching at the community college level. You might be able to give them some idea of the general academic atmosphere, the nature of the student body, and what the students expect from the faculty. These are just three examples of entirely different speeches in the same subject area, each designed for the interests of a specific audience.

In order to provide the kind of information your audience will want to have, there are several things you should try to find out about them.

Occupation or profession This is fairly easy to find out, because it is often the basis of the organization you are asked to address. If you know that you will be speaking to a group of businessmen, or doctors, or ski enthusiasts, you have some idea of the general interests that have brought the group together to begin with. Some of the members of a ski group might be interested in the newest treatment for glaucoma, but the group as a whole is not likely to be—although they might be interested in the newest techniques for setting broken legs. An audience of doctors might be only remotely interested in a discussion of mass-media advertising.

Suppose you can't find out? What if the person who invited you to speak knows only that the group has expressed interest in the subject and has no idea what they know or don't know about it. Don't just guess and hope for the best. Plan a speech that would have appeal for experts and beginners alike. If your subject is skiing, you don't have to decide whether to talk about the equipment a "snow bunny" needs or whether to talk about the execution of a high-speed parallel turn. Both beginners and experts might enjoy an illustrated lecture of the resorts and facilities of European skiing. If your subject is computers, both the layman and the professional might be interested in the possible uses of computers in business, science, and education.

Level of experience If you have been invited to speak on a specific topic (which is most frequently the case), try to find out what the group already knows about it. If you are the speaker, you are supposed to be the expert. You may find yourself in an embarrassing spot if you learn after your speech that the audience knew more about your subject than you did. You may know enough about heart transplants to provide useful information to a group of laymen, but perhaps not to a group of surgeons. They might be impressed, however, by your knowledge of back-packing or gourmet cooking.

If your speech is one of a series, find out what ideas were advanced in earlier speeches so that you can make specific reference to them. Try to work into your speech some activity that is of particular concern to your audience. If your speech is on the techniques of conducting a group discussion, ask whether any group discussions are planned for later programs. If so, select examples that your audience can apply in the actual situations that will confront them. Real examples are best, but hypothetical ones will serve.

The predominant sex   You should find out whether your audience will be predominantly male or female. This is no longer a major factor in audience analysis, especially with a young audience. However, it may affect your selection of topic, and especially any anecdotes you use. An all-male audience probably wouldn't appreciate a speech on beauty tips, nor would a female audience be especially interested in a talk on automobile mechanics (except in rare circumstances). Studies have shown, however, that in general a female audience adapts to a masculine topic more easily than a male audience adapts to a feminine topic.

The important thing is to anticipate as well as you can what kind of information your audience will want to have. It is possible, of course, to make some adjustments after you start talking, but this is difficult to do unless you are very experienced. For now, the best procedure is to plan your speech as well as you can, and then give it the way you planned it.

WILL THE AUDIENCE UNDERSTAND YOU?

Once you have determined what information your audience wants, you will have to consider the best way to communicate it to them. So far you have been addressing your classroom audience in the same way you would want to be addressed. However, in speaking to other kinds of audiences you might have to make adjustments in your presentation to be sure you are understood. There are two factors in particular that you should take into consideration.

The average age   The generation gap certainly isn't a new phenomenon. There have always been communication problems between the "old folks" and "young people with their new-fangled ideas." However, the present generation gap is probably somewhat greater than that between previous generations. So much has happened so fast in the last few decades that your world is vastly different from the one in which your parents grew up. Just stop to think that Orville Wright, who made the first flight at Kitty Hawk, died only nine years before the first artificial satellite was launched —and the new Boeing 747 is six feet longer than the flight he made. No other generation has had so much change or such different sets of values to try to adjust to.

Some of the barriers to communication, then, stem from a different perspective of the world. Your parents may have acute recollections of the depression days, but the possibility of a population explosion and world famine did not seem a very real problem to them. They were concerned about making their own way in a world that was basically secure; yours is the first generation in history to have really serious doubts about the survival of humanity. Some of them may have lived it up on bootleg liquor, but marijuana was smoked only by criminals, degenerates, and "dope fiends."

In addition to these *attitudinal* barriers to communication, there are also *linguistic* barriers. To your parents being "stoned" probably means being drunk, a "joint" is a cheap saloon, and being "busted" means being out of money.

The attitudinal barriers are not easy to deal with. Any one of them, in fact, might in itself be the topic of a speech to convince. Attitudes can't simply be dismissed, however, any more than the other side of any controversial issue can be ignored or dismissed.

The linguistic barriers are somewhat easier to surmount. They can usually be overcome by using standard English and avoiding generational colloquialisms. This doesn't mean using big words to impress your audience; it means using words that are accurate and are most likely to have the same meaning to both you and your audience. Slang expressions and the vernacular of a particular region or generation can be colorful and effective, but such terms are more frequently misunderstood than you think. Try listing some current expressions that "everybody uses" and see how much disagreement there is in your own class on the exact meaning of each one.

Educational level   It might be a bit difficult to determine the educational level of your audience, but you should try to estimate it. This will be an important factor in determining the level of your vocabulary and the complexity of your sentence structure. It is just as bad to talk down to an audience as it is to talk over their heads. The formal education of your audience will also influence the examples you use. Literary and historical allusions can lend color and interest to your speech, but only if your audience understands and appreciates them. The exploits of Paul Bunyan or Don Quixote will probably be familiar to most people, but a reference to Hecuba may be recognized by only a very specialized audience. Don't make the mistake of assuming, however, that a lack of formal education is necessarily an indication of ignorance. Some very well-read people have never gotten past high school—and by the same token, many haven't opened a book since they got out of college.

WILL THE AUDIENCE ACCEPT WHAT YOU SAY?

Even if you have planned a speech that your audience will understand, the attitudes and opinions they already hold will influence both the message they receive and their willingness to accept what you tell them. Speaking to an audience that has strong sentiments you don't know about is the best way to put your foot in your mouth—and you may be lucky to get off that easily. If you lightly dismiss a point your audience considers evidence they may not accept your thesis, but if you lightly dismiss some cherished belief or strong opinion you can get yourself in real trouble. These audience factors are difficult to determine and even more difficult to deal with. The important point is that any of them can automatically put you in the position of giving a speech to convince, regardless of the speech purpose you intended.

Political sentiments   There was a time when politics was one of the topics to be avoided in social discourse. It's a matter for speculation whether people are more open-minded now, but for the most part they will probably listen to what you say even if they disagree. If would behoove you, however, to find out whether or not they will disagree. Organizations such as the American Legion, the NAACP, the John Birch Society, the ACLU, and the Black Panthers have received enough publicity that you should know pretty well where they stand on current issues. If you are uncertain about the sentiments of some prominent organization, a volume called the *Encyclopedia of Associations* will give you some information about each one; it also gives the name and address of the executive secretary, who can provide you with further information.

Sometimes political leanings can be estimated from occupational or group associations. For example, you can generally assume that union members will be opposed to right-to-work legislation, teachers will favor aid-to-education programs, businessmen will support corporate-tax re-

ductions, police officers will be critical of restrictions on arrest procedures, and so on. There are times, however, when group association
doesn't tell the whole story. Suppose you were asked to speak to the
Young Republicans of your state on the subject of a guaranteed income.
You might assume that this issue would be supported only by very liberal
Democrats, but the fact of the matter is that one of the original propo-
nents was Milton Friedman, economic adviser to Barry Goldwater. By the
same token, the "no-knock" law, whereby narcotics agents no longer
need a search warrant to enter a premises, was enacted by a Democratic
congress.

As far as that goes, even the terms "liberal" and "conservative" may
not provide much guidance to a group's sentiments on a particular issue.
As many liberal as conservative groups have opposed specific civil-rights
legislation, and both may, for different reasons, support either position on
the war in Vietnam.

Be sure you know whether your audience has some stand on the issue
you are discussing. You will have to know whether you are giving a
speech to inform or a speech to convince.

Religious beliefs   It isn't likely that you will be asking anyone in the audience to
change his religion, but if you are addressing a group with specific religious convictions you had better know what those convictions are. They
would certainly be a factor, for example, if you were speaking on fluoridation of water to an audience of Christian Scientists, or on the preparation
of roast suckling pig to an audience of Orthodox Jews, or on the advantages of tub baths over showers to an audience of Moslems. In this kind
of situation you are dealing not with just one idea, but with an entire set
of values and beliefs which may be fundamental to your listeners' way of
life. Convictions of this nature are not limited to the organized religions.
You might expect the same factors to apply if you were talking about
teleportation to a group of scientists, or explaining the use of the bayonet
in hand-to-hand combat to a group of conscientious objectors.

You can't realistically expect your audience to change an entire way
of life on the basis of your short speech. How, then, do you deal with
topics that touch on religious convictions? First of all, you might look for
some common ground for acceptance of your thesis and base your case
on points that are not in direct opposition to the convictions of your
audience. For example, instead of trying to convince a Catholic audience
to change its attitude toward abortion, you might recommend that this
should be a matter for decision by the individual and the church rather

than the state. You might also have to refrain from a "hard-sell" approach and present your arguments only as matters for the audience to consider. In other words, if you are sincerely interested in accomplishing your goals, you may get further by settling for something less than categorical acceptance of your ideas. Do you think you would be compromising your principles in doing this? Would you consider it a compromise to base a case for immediate school desegregation on compliance with the federal law and not on equal rights, as some Southern governors have done? This is a point you may want to discuss in class.

Racial and cultural prejudice   There was a time when no man could win an election in Boston unless he had an Irish name; some people will not even listen to a speaker who has long hair or a beard; others judge a speaker's knowledge and ability by the color of his skin. Convictions based on prejudice are often deep-seated—and just as often they are hidden. People do not like to think that they are prejudiced. They prefer to see themselves as rational beings who base their judgments on facts. As a result, they are often not aware themselves of the biases that influence their acceptance or rejection of a speaker's ideas.

Politicians as a group are acutely aware of this factor in their audiences, and of course many of them have exploited it for their own ends. One of the techniques they have used to cut across racial and cultural boundaries is to find some means of linking themselves to the group they are addressing, some area in which the audience can identify with them as "one of their own kind." The fact that this has sometimes been done with little regard for integrity doesn't invalidate the technique itself as an effective means of overcoming what can be a serious barrier to communication. Whether we like it or not, prejudices do exist, and the speaker who fails to take them into consideration is unable to deal with them. The unscrupulous may take advantage of them; the sincere will treat them honestly; but only the naïve will ignore them.

Attitude toward the topic   Even if you ask a person what his attitude is on some topic you can't rely on his answer. Sometimes he will be unwilling to tell you his real attitude. Often, however, he will not be aware of it himself. This is another area that involves the self-image. People are concerned with the impression they make on others, but they are even more concerned with their images of themselves. A person who considers himself intelligent and cultured might tell you he enjoys opera, but you may be sadly disappointed in his actual response to a speech on this topic. A person who sees himself as a "free thinker" may surprise you with his resistance to liberal ideas. You can't count on people being open-minded on a controversial issue just because they said they were.

Whether your speech is expository or persuasive, a favorable attitude toward your topic is something you have to earn. Look again at what was said in Chapter 3 about the importance of your introduction. Remember, too, that when your topic is controversial and you don't know the attitudes of the audience, you have to start with the assumption that they are opposed to what you are advocating. If they are opposed, you will need this effort to gain their interest and favor; if they aren't opposed, reinforcing their favorable attitude may move them further toward action.

In most cases, because of the individual factors involved, the attitudes of the audience will be mixed. Moreover, because of the subtlety of these factors, negative attitudes are often not even apparent until after you have started speaking.

The captive audience   A captive audience is one that has not come to hear the speaker out of choice. Your classroom audience is an example. You have probably noticed by now that a captive audience is pretty hard to reach. They haven't come to hear you out of interest in your topic. In fact, if they resent having to be there, they may have come prepared to reject anything you have to say. Conversely, the members of a voluntary audience are interested to begin with, or they wouldn't have come. They are already receptive to the speaker's ideas because they want to feel that their decision to come was a good one and that their time has been well spent.

To test the theory that a voluntary audience is more likely than a captive audience to accept a speaker's ideas, all the students in a speech course were surveyed on their attitudes on extrasensory perception. Half the students were then required to attend a guest lecture on ESP given by Dr. Rhine of Duke University; attendance was optional for the other half of the students. A survey taken after the lecture showed that those who had attended voluntarily had moved closer to acceptance of ESP, whereas the views of the captive audience had remained pretty much the same. Of course, those who had gone voluntarily probably did so because they were more inclined to the speaker's ideas to begin with. However, the results do seem to indicate that people can be persuaded only when they are ready and willing to be persuaded.

Numerous audience factors will determine the audience's perception of you and your message, and in many cases what they perceive may not be at all what you intended to project. However, regardless of your own intentions, the message is the message received. If what you say is misconstrued or rejected, it may well be through no fault in your speech. But whatever the reason, the fact remains that the audience received the message as they did, and for them that is the message.

QUESTIONS FOR DISCUSSION

1 Do you think that slanting your material to a particular audience is dishonest? Under what circumstances? Under what circumstances is it advantageous to the audience?

2 Do you think age is the primary factor in the generation gap? You have probably heard some men say, "I'll never understand women." Why do you think men and women have trouble communicating with each other?

3 Would you say that people were more open-minded about political issues than about religious issues? Can you think of any situations in which the reverse might be true?

4 Is it a compromise of principle for a speaker to base his argument on some ground other than the one he himself considers the primary issue? Would you say that this was an evasion of the issue? Do you think it is a compromise of principle for a speaker to aim for anything less than complete acceptance of his ideas?

5 Are there any differences in the way a speaker might deal with open prejudice and hidden prejudice? Do you often judge a person's attitudes by his regional accent?

6 If a speaker can expect no more than to be heard out, is there any point in his speaking at all?

STUDY GUIDE

I. Before you take the first step in preparing any speech consider the audience you are to address.
   A. Find out as much as you can about your audience from the person who has asked you to speak.
   B. Be sure you know the size of the group, the type of occasion, the available facilities, and the type and length of speech you are expected to give.
II. Tailor your topic to the interests of your audience.
   A. Their occupation or profession is a clue to their general interests.

B. The level of their experience is a factor in determining what aspects of your topic to discuss.

C. The predominant sex may affect your general approach.

III. Adjust your presentation to be sure you will be understood.

A. The average age of the audience may be a clue to attitudinal and linguistic barriers.

B. Educational level is a factor in the sophistication of your vocabulary, sentence structure, examples.

IV. Find out whether the audience has strong sentiments that may bear on their acceptance of what you say.

A. Political leanings can sometimes be estimated from group association, but stands on specific issues should always be investigated.

B. Topics that touch on religious convictions concern not just one idea, but an entire set of fundamental values.

1. Try to base your thesis on some ground other than one that is in direct conflict with the convictions of your audience.

2. Be realistic in what you can expect your audience to accept.

C. Racial and cultural prejudices can sometimes be surmounted by finding some other area in which the audience can identify with you.

D. Real attitudes toward the topic may be quite different from the attitudes that are professed.

E. A captive audience is less receptive to a speaker's ideas than an audience whose attendance is voluntary.

CHAPTER 11

The message from your audience

In your first attempts at public speaking you probably had all you could do to concentrate on what you were saying to your audience without having to worry about what they were saying to you. As you gain experience and become more confident in yourself, you can start giving some thought to the message from your audience. In some cases you may be able to make spontaneous adjustments to them as you observe their reaction. Be careful, however, about going off on some tangent that you had not planned. It can take you farther afield than you thought when you began. Just as good impromptu speaking is not really impromptu, in the sense that it is based on a backlog of experience, effective spontaneous adjustments require a certain amount of forethought.

Before we discuss the more subtle aspects of adjusting to an audience, let's examine the area in which their response will be the most apparent.

THE QUESTION PERIOD

Most of your speeches will probably be followed by a question period. This can be the most challenging aspect of a speech, and perhaps the most fruitful in terms of communication. It is also the best way for you to find out how your audience reacted to what you had to say. Just as there are guidelines for making your prepared message effective, so there are guidelines for handling a question period:

Be sure there is no break in your relationship with the audience. The question period is just as much a part of your speech as the prepared portion. Don't deliver your speech with polished formality and then take the attitude during the question period that now you can relax and really talk to your audience. This is what you were supposed to have been doing all along.

Be sure you are armed with plenty of information on your subject. It is at this time that your audience will not only have a chance to clarify any points of confusion, but will also be able to find out if you really know what you are talking about. You should be able to add new information and use different examples in your replies, so that you aren't just rehashing what you have already said.

Anticipate as many of the questions as you can. If you are well prepared there should be few questions that take you by surprise. It is especially important in a speech to convince that you be prepared for questions and objections based on the opposing view. Don't let the audience think you have been caught off guard by a challenging question. Let them know that you welcome the opportunity to clarify your point.

Direct your answers to the whole audience. Don't address your response only to the person who asked the question. Remember that the question period is part of your speech, and you are speaking to the whole audience. First of all, make sure everyone has heard the question; if you have any doubt about this, repeat the question so they *can* hear it (and have the questioner confirm your paraphrase). Then answer so that everyone can hear. This problem arises most frequently when the questioner is sitting in the front row—and the people in the front row are the ones most likely to ask questions.

Be succinct. This applies just as much to your response to a question as to the prepared portion of your speech. A long-winded dissertation in reply to one question is uncalled for and inappropriate. It has the effect of discouraging others from asking questions.

Get lots of people involved. The question period should be dynamic; it should move rapidly and involve as many people as there is time for. There is always someone in the audience who will want to make a speech of his own, or will ask you one question after another. Don't let him. You may even have to interrupt him once you get the gist of his question. Answer it and then move on to someone else. If you get caught in a dialog with one person, you will lose the rest.

Stay on top of the situation. The question period is part of the public-speaking situation, not a group discussion. You should get lots of people involved, but be sure they don't take over the situation and start addressing questions to each other rather than to you. This can easily happen if you allow long questions or fail to reply to each question. If you notice private exchanges beginning to develop between members of the audience, this is the time to make a strong point as emphatically as you can to regain their attention. If it doesn't work, you might as well sit down.

Know when to stop. Since the question period is an important part of your speech, be sure you allow enough time for it. The length of a question period depends entirely on the circumstances. Often there are time limitations; other speakers may be scheduled or your audience may be on their lunch hour. If your time is not restricted, you will have to judge how long to allow questions to continue. As long as the whole audience seems interested, keep going, but don't let one or two questioners drag things on until the rest get bored. Try to get in the last word yourself, it's not a bad idea to save some closing remark as an exit line.

INDICATORS OF AUDIENCE RESPONSE

An audience will always give you some kind of feedback during your speech, either directly or indirectly. However, it is not always easy to interpret.

Overt response   There are certain traditional ways in which an audience demonstrates its response to a speaker. The most direct response is that strange custom of beating the hands together to show approval and appreciation. Applause in fact serves a very useful purpose. First of all, it unites the audience in a common activity and allows a large group of people to participate simultaneously in the communication process; they are all saying something together. Second, it gives the speaker concrete evidence of where he stands. One of the frightening things about facing an audience is that you don't really know how they are going to take you. A round of applause reassures you that you are among friends. Laughter when you tell a joke has the same effect; it lets you know that the audience is with you. This kind of overt response does a lot to put both the speaker and the audience at ease.

Covert response   While some kinds of audience response are unmistakable in meaning, there are also covert responses. Some are easier to spot than others, but not necessarily any easier to interpret. Yawning, whispered conversations, nodding, or shaking of the head may indicate individual reactions, but they don't tell much about the audience as a whole. And as individual reactions, they may be deceiving. A person who is yawning or has his eyes closed may be listening more intently than someone who looks wide awake. The girl in the second row who keeps nodding her head may not actually be expressing agreement; she may just be trying to follow what you are saying.

What message would you get when people in the audience are squirming around in their seats? You must have been told as a child to "sit still and pay attention." Is there actually any correlation between sitting still and paying attention? There is at least some evidence that there may be a connection. In one study the seats in an auditorium were outfitted with a "wiggle meter," which recorded any movements of the occupants. A number of audiences were subjected to different kinds of speeches, some dull and some interesting. The wiggle meter registered more movement during the dull speeches than during the interesting ones.[1]

You have probably also heard people say they could tell what someone was thinking by the expression on his face. This may not be a reliable index. Some people's faces habitually fall into a smile or a frown in repose. A knitting of the brows could mean either that the listener is trying hard to understand you or that he is skeptical about what you are saying. A grin on someone's face could indicate approval, or simply that he has noticed a gravy spot on your tie; he may even have been thinking about something totally different that happened to amuse him at that point. You should be aware of facial expressions, but recognize their limitations as measures of audience response.

[1]Elwood A. Kretsinger, "An Experimental Study of Gross Bodily Movement as an Index to Audience Interest," *Speech Monographs*, vol. 14, Nov., 1952.

For that matter, recent studies made with an "eye camera" have turned up an interesting point about dilation of the pupils. Apparently with a pleasing stimulus the pupils dilate and with a displeasing one they contract. Perhaps you are sensitive enough (or your sight is keen enough) to detect this phenomenon in your audience.

DEALING WITH AN INATTENTIVE AUDIENCE

Suppose you find that despite your most careful preparation in terms of audience interest, your audience still isn't attentive? What can you do about it?

The listener's state of mind   This is an aspect of audience attention over which you have no control. Even if you could find out all the things that were running through the minds of all the people in your audience, you couldn't do anything about them. Take just one member of the audience. As he left for school his landlady told him he was going to be evicted for back rent; he dented a fender on his father's car and the insurance had expired; his biology teacher said he was failing the course; and he just received notice from the draft board to report for his physical. He is likely to have a lot more on his mind than your speech on the natural habitat of the red-headed woodpecker.

The mood of the audience   Sometimes there are external factors that affect the mood of the entire audience. In November, 1963, a few hours before the opening of a week-long national conference of a branch of the American Psychological Association, the news of President Kennedy's assassination reached the public. This was an audience vitally interested in the subject, who had traveled from all parts of the country just to attend. Most of the speakers tried to go on with the speeches they had planned because they didn't know what else to do, but it's unlikely that even they were paying much attention to what they said. You may never be confronted with a situation of this magnitude, but there will be times when it is pointless to try to compete with the mood of your audience.

Environmental conditions   Here you have some control, although it may be limited. Before you begin speaking you should check to see that the physical situation is as favorable as possible. During your speech, however, you may have to deal with changes in the situation. For example, a room that was airy and comfortable when you began may become hot and stuffy

The message
The speaker
The audience

after it has been full of people for a while. You might be able to have someone turn down the thermostat or open a window.

You may find yourself having to cope with unanticipated noise. In general, if the noise is louder than you are, don't try to compete with it. If it is going to be of short duration—say, a plane overhead—the best thing to do is just stop talking and wait it out. If someone is operating a jackhammer right outside the door, you will have to take more positive measures. Having someone close the door may help, but you might have to ask the worker if he can stop until you are finished.

Distractions from the audience   Latecomers sometimes attract attention by their efforts to find seats. You may want to stop briefly to help them get settled, but try not to embarrass them by directing all eyes their way—and away from you. A more difficult problem to deal with is whispered conversations in the audience while you are speaking. To begin with, you are more likely to be distracted by this situation than your audience, since you are facing the whisperers, but the audience is facing you. If no one else is being distracted, it may be better to ignore the situation than to divert the attention of the rest of your audience. If you can catch the eye of the offenders discreetly, do so. In fact, if the people around them are being disturbed they may do this themselves. If the interference is too great, you may have to do something about it. One thing to bear in mind, however, is that an admonishment of one member of the audience may affect your rapport with the rest. The members of an audience tend to identify more with each other than with the speaker, and a reprimand of one constitutes a threat to the entire group.

You will have to invent your own system for handling such situations, and often it will have to be done spontaneously. The more experience you acquire, the easier it will get. To a large extent, the success of what you do will depend on the rapport you have established with your audience.

The quality of the stimulus   This is the aspect of attention over which you have the most control. Audiences are in an essentially passive position, and as a result, their attention will be drawn to whatever stimulus is the strongest. If your material is interesting and you deliver it well, you should be able to compete against the stimulus of most minor distractions. The next time you are in an auditorium or a classroom check for yourself how intently the audience is listening. If you see a lot of heads turning when there is a slight noise or someone gets up to leave, that's a sign that the stimulus provided by the speaker isn't strong enough to screen out small disruptions.

AUDIENCE RETENTION

There are some speakers who can hold their audiences rapt in the face of nearly all distractions, but they are few and far between. You are going to have to be realistic about the amount of attention you can expect. Not every word you utter is going to be remembered by posterity. In fact, studies show that immediately after a speech a person remembers only about half of what he has heard, and two months later he will have retained no more than one-quarter. You are going to have to decide, then, what quarter you want your listeners to retain. Some things you have to say are more important than others, and it's up to you to see that these are the points that are remembered. Even under the best of circum- stances your listeners may shunt aside the important information and absorb the trivial, but there are some things you can do to mimimize this possibility.

Suppose you consider some statement vital and you want to make sure that your audience will recognize its significance and remember it. How can you emphasize it so that it stands out from the rest of your material? There are several ways a printed sentence might be emphasized: it can be underlined, set off by an exclamation point, displayed on a separate line, or printed in italics or boldface. You can't do any of these things with a spoken sentence. However, there are other ways in which you can emphasize spoken sentences. Let's turn again to the studies.[2]

Position The placement of the statement in the speech is one factor in audience retention. Although the evidence is subject to qualification, it appears that audiences are most likely to remember what you say first and what you say last. Plan your introduction and your conclusion carefully to take full advantage of these two vital areas of the speech. Audience attention is probably highest at the very beginning of the speech; it tapers off toward the middle and then picks up again when the audience senses that you are concluding. The points at which you have the greatest attention are the times to make your most significant statements.

Repetition This appears to be the most effective mode of emphasis. The studies indicate that a statement repeated three to five times in a speech is generally remembered. This may be a bit too much in a short speech, but it does give you some idea. Repetition may be either *concentrated* or

[2]Arthur A. Jersild, "Modes of Emphasis," *Journal of Applied Psychology,* vol. 10, no. 6, pp. 611–620, 1928.

distributed. If you were using concentrated repetition you might repeat your statement in different words:

> The population of the world will double in the next thirty years. There will be twice as many people on our planet in the year 2000.

Or you might restate it in exactly the same words, perhaps with different inflection. If you distribute your repetition at different points in the speech, the impact is greater if you restate it in the same words, with strong vocal emphasis.

Look at the use of restatement in these memorable words by Winston Churchill:

> We shall defend our island, whatever the cost may be. We shall fight on the beaches. We shall fight on the landing grounds. We shall fight in the fields and in the streets, and we shall fight in the hills. We shall never surrender.

The pointer phrase   One exceedingly effective way to emphasize an important statement is simply to announce that you are about to make an important statement. Consider your own reaction when an instructor says

> Now, this is important and will probably be included on the final examination.

If you can, include the reason the point to follow is important:

> One point stands out, and this is something that will affect us all within our own lifetime. Unless we can change the present trend, the population of the world will double in the next thirty years.

Be sure, however, that the statement you are pointing to is truly significant, and that it is stated in such a way that it can be remembered easily.

Oratorical emphasis   The methods we have discussed so far apply to written statements as well as to spoken ones. However, there are some modes of emphasis that are available only to a speaker. They include such things as dramatic pauses, changes in vocal inflection and volume, movement and gestures—in short, all the methods and techniques we discussed in Chapter 9. As a speaker you have access not only to verbal communication, but to all the methods of nonverbal communication as well. You might consider such devices a bit "hammy," but they are the same things you would do spontaneously in any other situation. Employing them purposely does not make them less legitimate as a means of communication as long as your purpose itself is a legitimate one.

If you accept the contention that people can believe a falsehood as easily as they can believe a truth, it follows that the message they receive depends to a large extent on the skill of the speaker. Truth and justice are not self-evident. The only way they can prevail is if they are advocated by honest and just men who are effective in their communication. Sixteen hundred years ago St. Augustine wrote:[3]

> Who will dare to say that truth in the person of its defenders is to take its stand unarmed against falsehood. . . . Are those who are trying to persuade men of what is false to know how to introduce their subject, so as to put the hearer into a friendly, or attentive, or teachable frame of mind, while the defenders of the truth shall be ignorant of that art? That the former are to tell their falsehoods briefly, clearly, and plausibly, while the latter shall tell the truth in such a way that it is tedious to listen to, hard to understand, and, in fine, not easy to believe. . . . Who is such a fool as to think this wisdom?

QUESTIONS FOR DISCUSSION

1 How reliably can you judge a person's reaction by the look on his face? Which of the covert responses would you say was the most reliable indication?

2 If you found after you began to speak that your audience was not interested in what you were saying, what would you do about it?

3 What are some of the ways in which a speaker can deal with distractions in the audience? What methods do you think might be effective for you? How would you deal with a deliberate heckler?

4 Would you consider it ethical to stimulate an audience by planting people to applaud? Where would you draw the line between legitimate persuasion and manipulation?

5 Can an intelligent audience always pick out the important points of any speech? What purpose does oratorical emphasis serve?

6 Do you believe that truth requires the same kind and amount of support from a speaker as falsehood, or do you feel that truth is its own defense?

[3] *On Christian Doctrine*, book IV, chap. 2, translated by J. F. Shaw, Great Books of the Western World, vol. 18, Encyclopedia Britannica (William Benton, Publisher), Chicago, 1952.

STUDY GUIDE

   I. During the question period you will be able to find out how the audience has reacted to your speech.
     A. Treat the question period as part of the public-speaking situation.
     B. Have plenty of information, anticipate questions, and utilize the opportunity to reinforce your main ideas.
     C. Involve the whole audience, keep things moving, and know when to stop.
  II. The audience will provide you with continual feedback during your speech.
     A. Overt responses help to put both you and the audience at ease.
     B. Covert responses are difficult to interpret with any reliability.
 III. You can deal with some aspects of audience attention during your speech.
     A. Be alert to environmental distractions.
     B. In dealing with distractions from members of the audience be careful not to divert attention from yourself or jeopardize your rapport with the rest of your audience.
     C. Be sure the stimulus of your material is strong enough to screen out most minor distractions.
 IV. The points you emphasize are the ones your audience is most likely to retain.
     A. Make your most significant points at the beginning and the end of your speech.
     B. Use either concentrated or distributed repetition of important points.
     C. Utilize the pointer phrase to introduce important statements.
     D. Employ all the methods of nonverbal communication and vocal emphasis to point up important statements.
  V. Truth and justice are not self-evident; they will prevail only if they are advocated effectively by the honest and just.

Index

The message
The speaker
The audience

The message
The speaker
The audience

The message
The speaker
The audience